War among the Clouds

New Brunswick Airmen in the Great War

J. Brent Wilson

T0272136

Goose Lane Editions and the Gregg Centre for the Study of War and Society

Edited by Marc Milner.
Copy edited by Barry Norris.
Cover and page design by Julie Scriver.
Maps by Mike Bechthold.
Cover illustration: Lieutenant Alfred Belliveau in front
of a Sopwith Camel at Dover airfield, England, 1917.
P37-B021, Centre d'études acadiennes Anselme-
Chiasson, Université de Moncton
Printed in Canada by Friesens.
10 9 8 7 6 5 4 3 2 1

Goose Lane Editions acknowledges the generous
support of the Government of Canada, the Canada
Council for the Arts, and the Government of
New Brunswick.

Goose Lane Editions and the Gregg Centre for
the Study of War and Society at the University of
New Brunswick are located on the unceded territory
of the Wəlastəkwiyik whose ancestors along with the
Mi'kmaq and Peskotomuhkati Nations signed Peace
and Friendship Treaties with the British Crown in
the 1700s.

Goose Lane Editions
500 Beaverbrook Court, Suite 330
Fredericton, New Brunswick
CANADA E3B 5Y4
gooselane.com

Library and Archives Canada Cataloguing
in Publication

Title: War among the clouds : New Brunswick
airmen in the Great War / J. Brent Wilson. Other
titles: New Brunswick airmen in the Great War
Names: Wilson, J. Brent, author.
Series: New Brunswick military heritage series ;
v. 31.
Description: Series statement: New Brunswick
military heritage series ; v. 31 | Includes
bibliographical references and index.
Identifiers: Canadiana 20240346300 |
ISBN 9781773104294 (softcover)
Subjects: LCSH: Great Britain. Royal Air Force. |
LCSH: World War, 1914-1918—Aerial
operations, British. | LCSH: World War,
1914-1918—Personal narratives, Canadian. |
LCSH: Airmen—New Brunswick—Biography. |
LCGFT: Biographies.
Classification: LCC UG626 .W55 2024 | DDC
358.40092/27151—dc23

New Brunswick Military Heritage Project
The Brigadier Milton F. Gregg, VC,
Centre for the Study of War and Society
University of New Brunswick
PO Box 4400
Fredericton, New Brunswick
CANADA E3B 5A3
unb.ca/nbmhpw

Dedicated to the New Brunswick airmen who served in the British air services and Canadian Air Force during the Great War.

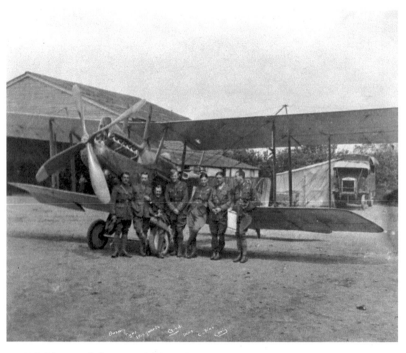

RE.8A aircraft from No. 35 Squadron, Savy-Berlette, France, May 15, 1917;
Lieutenant Alvah Good from Fredericton, NB (centre). MC 300/MS 69/23, PANB.

Contents

Introduction

Air operations during the Great War of 1914–18 added a new dimension to modern warfare. At the time, flying in powered aircraft was relatively new; many people had never seen an airplane, let alone flown in one. The famous Wright Brothers made the first airplane flight in the United States in December 1903 when Orville went twenty feet in the air, stayed aloft for twelve seconds, and then landed 120 feet away from his starting position. That was only eleven years before the beginning of the war. Like many modern wars, the Great War created rapid change, especially when it came to technology, and accelerated changes already taking place. By the time the conflict ended in 1918, airmen and their aircraft had done almost everything they ever would in wartime.

Nevertheless, air operations during the Great War were about much more than technological change—the individuals using this new knowledge were also deeply affected by their experiences. This book focuses on the almost three hundred New Brunswickers who served in the British flying services, in the air (as pilots, observers, air gunners), on the ground (as mechanics who maintained and repaired the aircraft's frames, engines, and other equipment), and as instructors. Most who saw active service at the front fought in France and Belgium, but some served in the war's more far-flung theatres of operation, including Italy, Egypt, Macedonia, and Russia. Many others served in Britain or underwent training at home later in the war, when local recruiting and training became extensive.

This book coincides with the one hundredth anniversary of the founding of the Royal Canadian Air Force (RCAF) in 1924. Although a small Canadian air force comprised of a two-squadron wing attached to the Royal Air Force (RAF) was formed overseas in 1918, it never became operational. Most of the province's airmen served with the British air services from 1914 to early 1918; this meant the Royal Flying Corps (RFC) and the Royal Naval Air Service (RNAS), which were amalgamated on April 1, 1918, to form the RAF. Nevertheless, the RCAF recognizes these early airmen as part of Canada's wartime aviation tradition. Volume I of the RCAF's official history, *Canadian Airmen and the First World War*, lists more than twenty-two thousand Canadians who served in the British air services throughout the war. Among them was a small but significant group of airmen from across New Brunswick. Some served in the RCAF after the war, and a few fought again during the Second World War.

The book focuses on the personal experiences of these airmen and uses their own words whenever possible. It draws on various sources, including such official documents as personnel files found in the Air Ministry and Admiralty records in Britain's The National Archives, the Canadian Expeditionary Force (CEF) records at Library and Archives Canada, and the Canadian Armed Forces' Directorate of History in Ottawa. Other collections are found in local repositories, including the Provincial Archives of New Brunswick, the New Brunswick Museum, Centre d'études acadiennes Anselme-Chiasson, and other local museums and historical societies. Another valuable source is the numerous provincial newspapers, which closely followed the exploits of these airmen, especially the pilots and observers, throughout the war. Of particular interest are the letters written home to family by airmen that were printed verbatim in the papers. Many of these airmen were well-educated and literate, and wrote wonderfully descriptive accounts of their experiences. On a few occasions, access was gained to private collections still held by the families of the airmen.

Chapter One

Joining Up: Recruitment and Enlistment

The first step in becoming an airman in the British air services during the Great War was enlistment. New Brunswick airmen joined up for many different reasons. They also came from diverse backgrounds, especially later in the war when the size of the services grew dramatically. As well, they enlisted in ways that changed over time as the demand for both air crew (pilots, observers, and air gunners) and ground crew (mechanics) increased.

Motivations for Joining Up

New Brunswickers enlisted in the air war for different reasons, although few elucidated their motivations. Leonard Richardson, who was born on Deer Island in Charlotte County, wrote about the role of patriotism and a sense of duty. On February 12, 1918, while training in Scotland, Richardson stated in a letter to his mother: "it is my duty to fight and because you have given me, not to let you down. We all must give and work our damndest [*sic*] in order to ensure safety and peace to the coming generation." More pragmatically, William Allison Weldon Carter, who was born in Saint John but grew up in Fredericton, wrote after the war in the *University of New Brunswick Memorial Magazine*: "I thought that fighting in the air was much to be preferred to fighting on the ground.

Robert Shives (centre) and his family's 1910 Cadillac before the war.
Courtesy of Patti Craig

Consequently, I was highly elated when I received a letter saying my application for a commission in the Royal Naval Air Service had been accepted." Others were drawn to the modern technology of air warfare. In a letter to his parents printed in the *Daily Gleaner* on May 2, 1916, George Alvah Good from Fredericton stated shortly before joining the air service: "I'm very much enthused about it. I think the R.F.C. [Royal Flying Corps] is the place where I can be of most use, and my former experience [as a signalling and machine-gun officer] ought to be extremely valuable to me, and you know how interested I am in mechanical things." Robert Shives from Campbellton was interested in automobiles, and airplanes were probably an exciting next step.

For others, friendships and family connections seem to have played a part in their enlistment. Louis Ritchie and Clair Gilmour from Saint John both enlisted in the Canadian Expeditionary Force (CEF) in 1916 and then joined the RFC in 1917 and trained as observers. They had been

Sitting at left is Louis Ritchie (goalie); standing behind him is
Clair Gilmour from the 1909–10 Saint John High School hockey team.
Courtesy of Margot and David Russell

close friends from a young age, and had been teammates on the Saint John
High School hockey team. Gilmour married Nellie Williams, a childhood
friend of Ritchie's. Also joining the air services were several sets of brothers
and cousins, including Gerald, Thomas, and William Creaghan; Edward
and Talmage Hanning; Evan, James, and Robert McMillan; Morden and
Godfrey Mowat; George and Medlee Parlee; Harold and John Price; and
Harry and Robert Wyse.

Backgrounds
Many airmen were surprisingly young when they enlisted — pilots and
observers, especially, were mostly in their late teens and early twenties.
Cadet Charles Arthur Clark from Saint John was an eighteen-year-old
student when he joined up in May 1918, while Cadet J.A. Ernest Boudreau

from Campbellton was nineteen when he enlisted a few months later, in August. Mechanics, however, were often older—in their late twenties and thirties. For example, Omer Leon Steeves was a thirty-year-old salesman from Albert Mines in Albert County when he enlisted as a mechanic in the RFC on May 16, 1917.

They also came from diverse backgrounds. Early in the war, many, especially those who would become officers, came from prominent and affluent local families. Some came from the province's business community. For example, John T. Gibson from Marysville, near Fredericton, was the grandson of Alexander "Boss" Gibson, who built and operated the Marysville Cotton Mill, one of the largest of its kind in Canada; he was also involved in railroad development. The fathers of Robert Shives and Morden Mowat were prominent lumbering and milling businessmen on the North Shore. Both owned sawmills in the Campbellton area. Others came from families connected to the province's political and professional establishments. Josiah Wood, the father of William Trueman Wood, was a former lieutenant governor; Sir Pierre-Amand Landry, Wilfred Landry's father, was Chief Justice of the New Brunswick Supreme Court, and a former Member of Parliament (MP) and Member of the Legislative Assembly (MLA). The fathers of Gibson and David Mott of Campbellton were an MP and an MLA, respectively. Fredericton's Weldon Carter was the son of the chief superintendent of education for the province.

Others were employed in their own professional careers as engineers, lawyers, and teachers before the war. Franklin Rankin, from Woodstock, became a civil engineer after graduating from the Royal Military College in Kingston, Ontario, in May 1914. Harold Price from Moncton was an electrical engineer, while Joseph Arthur Cyr from Saint-Hilaire, Madawaska County, was a barrister. Byron McNally from Fredericton was a practising dentist in Alberta when he enlisted.

These prominent backgrounds were not coincidental. The British air services had high standards for enlistment. They were looking for officers and gentlemen, and the technical nature of the training required higher levels of education. Not surprisingly, therefore, many of these airmen were university students and graduates. John Gibson, Alvah Good, Hubert

Osborne, Talmage Hanning, Royden Smith, Robert Shives, and John Hanson all attended the University of New Brunswick (UNB). Charles Edgecombe and Hubert Osborne both went to the Wesleyan Academy, a private Methodist boy's school in Sackville. Edgecombe graduated from Mount Allison University, as did Albert Desbrisay Carter, Gordon Mott, and Evan McMillan. Alfred Belliveau attended high school and the first few years of a Bachelor of Arts program at the Collège Saint-Joseph, a liberal arts school in Memramcook run by priests from the Holy Cross Order; Aimé Léger also studied there. Robert Shives, Vernon Hatch, and Franklin Rankin went to the Rothesay Collegiate School, now known as the Rothesay Netherwood School.

Nevertheless, many airmen came from more diverse backgrounds, especially later in the war when recruitment became more intensive. For example, Charles Cawley from St. George, a carpenter before the war, enlisted as a private in the 11th Battalion in 1916 and later transferred to the RFC and was commissioned. Herbert Carrick Barr from Moncton was a chauffeur and mechanic, while Frederick Ward Ervine was a farmer from Andover.

Like others from across the country, most of New Brunswick's airmen were residents of the province's cities and towns, especially Saint John, Moncton, and Fredericton, as well as Campbellton, Bathurst, Chatham, Newcastle, St. Stephen, and Woodstock. As time went on, however, new enlistees also came from smaller communities, such as Rolling Dam Station, Flat Lands, Molus River, Coal Branch, Jacksonville, Bloomfield Station, Butternut Ridge, River Louison, and Milltown. Nevertheless, New Brunswick's large rural population and comparatively small urban centres likely help to explain the province's low representation among Canadian airmen.

Many of these airmen also had prior military service in the province's militia. Arthur Cyr, the barrister from Saint-Hilaire, had extensive experience in the militia before enlisting for overseas service in 1916. As the *Quarterly Militia Lists* show, he first joined the 67th Regiment (Carleton Light Infantry) in 1909 as a bugler and progressed quickly through the ranks, becoming a lieutenant in February 1913. He also served briefly with the 73rd Northumberland Regiment. In February 1916, he joined the 74th Regiment (The New Brunswick Rangers), with which he was serving when he enlisted in the 165th (Acadian) Battalion of the CEF in April 1916.

Enlistment

Throughout the war, New Brunswick's airmen enlisted in the British air services in three different ways: by obtaining a private civilian flying certificate; by secondment or transfer from CEF units overseas; or by direct enlistment in the RFC's training program in Canada. Early on, a few individuals privately obtained a civil aviation pilot's certificate in Canada, the United States, or Britain, and then applied to the air services. Once accepted, they went to Britain to undergo more advanced training. This was an expensive process, which also helps to explain why some airmen came from affluent backgrounds. Among them were Robert Shives and Morden Mowat, both from Campbellton, Lloyd Sands from Moncton, and Royden Foley from Saint John. In April 1915, Shives and Mowat attended the Curtiss School of Aviation at Long Branch in Toronto, likely at their own expense and, according to the *Campbellton Graphic*, shared a tent during training. Shives was born at Campbellton on July 20, 1891. His father, Kilgour, a prominent businessman in the area, was killed accidentally in 1905 and was buried in Fernhill Cemetery in Saint John, where he and his wife, Maria, had lived before moving to Campbellton. Robert was educated at the Campbellton Grammar School, and between 1909 and 1913 he attended UNB in Fredericton, where he earned a Bachelor of Science in forestry. Afterwards, he worked in the forest industry in the province with the New Brunswick Land and Railway Company. When war broke out in 1914, he tried to enlist but was turned down due to an ankle injury he had received while engaged in forestry work near Grand Falls. In April 1915, Robert began a four-month-long pilot training course at the Curtiss Aviation School. After graduating, he proceeded to England; in early October, he was made a second lieutenant in the RFC.

Morden Mowat was born on December 6, 1891, in New Westminster, British Columbia. His father, Maxwell Millidge Mowat, had moved from

Robert Shives and his aeronautical class. Courtesy of Patti Craig

Campbellton to British Columbia in 1880 looking for business opportunities. There he met and married Lillian Clarke from Toronto, and two sons, Morden and Oliver, were born in British Columbia before the family returned to Campbellton in 1895. Max entered into the lumber business with his brother and became a prominent member of the local community. Morden appears in the 1901 census as "Morgan," then nine years old and living with the family in Campbellton, but by 1911 he was no longer residing at home. In time, he moved to Cobalt, Ontario, where he joined the McKinley-Darragh Mining Company. In November 1915, the *Moncton Daily Times* reported that Mowat, now twenty-three, had become the fifty-eighth graduate of the Curtiss Aviation School. A few weeks later he left for England, and soon was attached to the RFC. On January 6, 1916, he joined No. 23 Squadron, and then on March 16 he transferred to No. 11 Squadron and shortly afterward became a flying officer.

Lloyd Sands attended flying school through other means. In 1915, he received a loan of $400 from the city of Moncton to pay for his enrollment in the Toronto aviation school. Later, after undergoing a preliminary training course at HMCS *Niobe* in Halifax, he became one of the first New Brunswickers to join the RNAS, enlisting on February 3, 1916, with

the rank of flight sub-lieutenant. On August 21, Sands completed his training in England on a Blériot monoplane at the Royal Naval Air Station at Redcar, Yorkshire, and then began active service in France.

Lastly, Royden Foley obtained an aero certificate in the United States prior to joining the air services. Born in Saint John in July 1891, Foley was educated at the Saint John High School and then, between 1913 and 1915, attended the Pratt Institute of Technology in New York City, where he studied engineering and became interested in flying. A newspaper article in the *Montreal Daily Star* written during the Second World War when Foley was a squadron leader in the Royal Canadian Air Force stated:

> The Wright brothers were installed at Mineola, Long Island, in 1912 [*sic*] when … Foley, then newly graduated from the Pratt Institute of Science and Technology, New York, turned up at the flying field one day to see what it was all about. He had a "craze" for aviation and had already been experimenting with gliders when he met the Wrights. Squadron Leader Foley points out that at that time the Wrights allowed anybody who felt an inclination to "tinker" with machines that had not turned out successfully to "play around with them." He seized the opportunity and, at the same time learned to pilot the rickety-looking machines of the day.

165th (Acadian) Battalion at Camp Valcartier, Quebec, 1916.
Moncton Museum Collection

On October 28, 1916, Foley obtained his aero certificate at the Wright Brothers School, flying a Wright biplane. Afterwards, he returned to Canada, and on November 5, 1917, the twenty-six-year-old Foley enlisted in the RFC Canada program in Toronto and underwent training at Fort Worth, Texas. In early 1918, he left for England, where he underwent further training and then joined No. 251 Squadron on active maritime operations.

Overseas Enlistment
Many others first joined units from the various branches of the CEF raised throughout the province, including the infantry, artillery, and engineers, and then transferred to the air services once they arrived overseas. Among the early soldiers who entered from the CEF was Captain Burpee McLeod Hay from Woodstock. An engineer in civil life before the war, Hay had served as an officer in the militia's 28th Dragoons since 1912. On September 22, 1914, he enlisted in the First Canadian Contingent's 1st Field Company, Canadian Engineers (CE), at Camp Valcartier, Quebec, and was promoted to captain. On October 3, he sailed for England, where he joined the engineering depot. On May 16, 1915, he was seconded to the RFC, becoming one of the province's earliest airmen of the Great War. Burdette Harmon, from the engineer company, later joined the RFC as well.

Several Acadians joined the air services. Six came from the 165th (Acadian) Battalion, raised throughout the Maritimes in 1916: Lieutenants Alfred Hilaire Belliveau, Joseph Arthur Cyr, Edgar Patrick LeBlanc, Aimé Léger, and Albert Melanson, and Private François (Frank) Gallant. Belliveau was born on September 28, 1894, in Fredericton, to Alphée Thomas and Marie (Babineau) Belliveau. Alphée was the head of the French department at the provincial Normal School, the provincial teachers' college of its day. Marie was a graduate of the program who taught in Fredericton until she married Alpheé and had children. Both parents were fluently bilingual and prominent members of the province's Acadian community, actively promoting their presence in New Brunswick. Alfred, the second youngest of seven children, attended St. Dunstan's elementary school in Fredericton, where he studied in French until 1910, when he went to high school and then university at the Collège Saint-Joseph in Memramcook, completing about two and a half years of his Bachelor of Arts degree before deciding to join Canada's effort in the Great War.

On February 11, 1916, Belliveau and fellow Saint-Joseph student Aimé Léger from Cocagne, Kent County, enlisted in Moncton in the newly formed 165th Battalion, Belliveau as a private. Prior to this Alfred had served in the militia's 67th Regiment for three years. He became a physical training instructor and drill instructor, was appointed company sergeant major, and sent to Halifax to take a course in physical training. Later, he undertook officer training in Halifax and, on September 20, 1916, was commissioned as a first lieutenant. The 165th moved to Saint John in 1916 and stationed in the armoury until early 1917, when they transferred to Camp Valcartier. Belliveau went to Toronto, where he attended an advanced course in physical training. He rapidly increased his strength and coordination, and — according to his memoir, "Thoughts in Old Age" — "some of us began to feel a little cocky." On March 28, 1917, Belliveau and the rest of the 165th sailed from Halifax to Liverpool on board the troopship *Metagama*. They were stationed at Shoreham-by-Sea, on the south coast near Brighton, until April 1917. However, as Belliveau wrote,

After a while, some of us began to suspect that the British Army did not know what to do with us. And sure enough, we were finally told our battalion was being transformed into a Forestry Battalion, to cut logs for trenches and dugouts.

This of course was a necessary activity, but proved a great disappointment to some. Lieutenant Aimé Léger, Lieutenant Arthur Cyr and myself then promptly applied for transfer to the British Royal Flying Corps, in August of 1917.

More future airmen came from several other CEF units raised in New Brunswick, including the 26th, 64th, 104th, 140th, and 236th Battalions.

Some New Brunswickers had already acquired extensive military experience at the front by the time they joined the air services. Foremost among them was Burdette William Harmon, who was born on April 3, 1888, in Peel, Carleton County, and lived in Woodstock. After attending high school in Woodstock, Harmon graduated from UNB in 1912 and became Assistant Inspector of Fish Hatcheries with the Dominion Marine and Fisheries Department. He was also a member of the militia's 1st (Brighton) Field Company, CE. At the outset of the war, he enlisted as a sapper in the First Contingent's 1st Field Company, CE, and sailed to England on October 3, 1914. He saw action during several of the CEF's early fights between the Second Battle of Ypres and Vimy Ridge. On June 15, 1915, he was wounded at Givenchy while serving in a bombing party with the 1st Battalion. The *London Gazette* citation for the Distinguished Conduct Medal (DCM) he was awarded described the action:

For conspicuous gallantry and devotion; he constructed a barricade with sandbags across a road under heavy fire, and kept repairing it, when partly demolished by heavy shell fire. Later he remained for thirty-six hours alone constructing tunnels. On another occasion he accompanied the assault in charge of a blocking party to barricade trenches gained. After the first line of trenches had been taken and nearly all the party killed or wounded, Sapper Harmon armed himself with bombs, and continued to force his way forward until he had exhausted the supply and could get no more. During the operations he was severely wounded in several places.

Harmon downplayed his role in the attack in a letter published in the Fredericton *Daily Gleaner* in August 1915. Nonetheless, the citation formed the basis for Sir Max Aitken's description of Harmon's actions in *Canada in Flanders*, published in 1916.

Harmon was evacuated to hospital in England. In mid-December 1915, he transferred to the infantry and was commissioned from the ranks as a lieutenant in the 52nd Battalion. In December 1916, the *Carleton Sentinel* reported that he had been awarded the Military Cross (MC) for "conspicuous gallantry in the Thelus Section on the 6th December 1916. Having on the morning of the 6th after blowing up 40 feet of wire, led a raiding party into the enemy's trench, bombed three dugouts inflicting many casualties on the enemy and brought two unwounded prisoners into our line." Then, in March 1917, Harmon received the Russian Cross of St. George. He was again wounded on April 17, 1917, at Vimy Ridge and hospitalized. In May 1917, Harmon transferred to the Royal Flying Corps.

Recruiting in Canada

The final way New Brunswickers entered the flying services was by direct enlistment in Canada. At the same time as soldiers in the CEF were volunteering for the air services overseas, men were being enlisted back home in Canada, especially as mechanics and other ground crew. Active recruiting in New Brunswick for mechanics began as early as March 1915, when Lieutenant-Colonel B.R. Armstrong, the province's chief recruiter, based in Saint John, received instructions to enlist volunteers for the RFC, which was looking for "skilled mechanics and those accustomed to flying machines and automobiles." By November 1915, the RFC's requirements for mechanic recruits had become more detailed. Articles in provincial newspapers outlined that, to qualify, candidates had to be under thirty years of age, medically fit for service overseas, be of "good character," be

Royal Flying Corps recruiting poster,
Moncton Daily Times, November 3, 1917.

a member of the required trades, and capable of performing a proficiency test. If they qualified, they would be enlisted for the duration of the war, initially as air mechanic 2nd class. Among the required trades were mechanical transport drivers, fitters, riggers, motor cyclists, carpenters, electricians, and sail makers. Pending classification once they reached England, their pay was $15 per month with additional free rations, clothing, and accommodations.

Then, at the beginning of 1917, recruiting in Canada became more comprehensive when the RFC set up a large-scale training establishment in Ontario at Camps Borden, Armour Heights at Leaside, and Long Branch around Toronto, Camps Mohawk and Rayburn at Deseronto, near Belleville in eastern Ontario, and later at Beamsville in the Niagara area. Mechanics were required to maintain the fleet of aircraft being built in Canada to train pilots for service with the RFC at the front. As early as the beginning of March 1917, advertisements appeared in eastern Canadian newspapers calling on tradesmen of all kinds to consider enlisting; among those needed were acetylene welders, blacksmiths, motor drivers, electricians, engine fitters, motor cycle fitters, millwrights, metal turners, tinsmiths, cabinet makers, and vulcanizers. Recruiters appealed to men who not only wanted to serve their country, but also those "with ambition, as after the war, they will be able to take their places as leaders in the different branches of the coming great transportation service, through the air." Another incentive was the higher rates of pay mechanics received, ranging from $1.10 per diem for air mechanics 3rd class to $2.50 for warrant officers. Married men also received a separation allowance. An additional incentive was that the percentage of non-commissioned officers (NCOs) in the RFC was higher than in the other military branches, so promotion was much quicker. The RFC's more relaxed medical standards also made enlistment easier for those who had failed medical tests elsewhere because of such things as flat feet and other minor physical defects. It was also made clear that mechanics would participate in ground duties only and would not be required to fly. "Their sole duties consist in keeping the machines in repair and running order at the different squadron headquarters and aerodromes, although there is nothing to prevent them if they so desire after being in the service, from applying for flight work, if they pass the necessary test."

Mechanics came from various backgrounds and training. Henry Evans of Saint John joined a construction corps at Toronto in April 1917 and, according to the *Saint John Globe*, "within a week was given an opportunity to undergo examination for the flying corps. He was successful in passing with high honors and was immediately sent to aviation headquarters." According to John D. Howe, a Saint John cabinet maker, Evans had been in his employ for about four years "and had become a very skillful workman. He considered the training that he had received in woodworking and metal repair work in his shop to be of a higher standard than was possible to be attained in a factory, and he was convinced that the young man, about twenty-one years of age, would be a success along the mechanical lines in the King's service or elsewhere."

When recruiting in Canada for both flying cadets and mechanics for the RFC opened in early 1917, the process became more localized. Prospective candidates were instructed to apply by letter to various locations throughout the country. For the Maritimes, they were directed to the recruiting officer at the Tramway Building in Halifax. Or they could contact members of local recruiting committees that were set up to assist the RFC, including E.A. Schofield in Saint John and W.H. Price at City Hall in Moncton. For flying cadets, the RFC was looking for men between the ages of eighteen and twenty-five "who were physically fit, and who were well educated," which meant having completed high school and at least two years of college, or having two years' experience in office work. Having met the requirements, candidates were eligible for a cadetship and would receive a course of training of from four to six months on Canadian aircraft at one of the three RFC stations in Canada. Upon completion they would be gazetted as lieutenants in the RFC and sent to England for further training and posting to operational squadrons. Successful New Brunswick candidates travelled to Halifax to attest before being sent to Toronto for training.

A potential challenge to recruiting for the air services arose in early 1918 with the enforcement of the Military Services Act. New regulations required that those who were eligible for the draft but still wanted to enlist in the air services first had to join their depot battalion and then transfer to the RFC after receiving their commanding officer's consent. Concern arose that this added step might deter potential RFC recruits. The *Daily Telegraph* patriotically concluded that "the fascination and romance attaching to the flying man's work appeal so strongly to the Canadian spirit that most men will be keen enough to make the extra effort to join." This proved to be the case in several instances in New Brunswick, where draftees who were called up and enrolled in the 1st Depot Battalion of the New Brunswick Regiment at Saint John received permission from Lieutenant-Colonel J.L. McAvity, the commanding officer, to volunteer for the RFC and, after being discharged, proceeded to Toronto for attestation. Among them were Air Mechanic 2nd Class Alfred Byron Atherton, a twenty-nine-year-old watchmaker from Woodstock, and flying cadets Bradstreet Tompkins from East Florenceville, James Wilfred McManus from West Bathurst, and Aimé LeBlanc from Saint-Anselme, near Moncton, each of whom underwent cadet training in Ontario. Tompkins, who was a twenty-year-old bookkeeper and stenographer, enlisted with the Depot

Battalion in Saint John on April 24, 1918, and was discharged on the same day so he could join the RAF, newly created on April 1 with the merger of the RFC and RNAS. He attested in Toronto on May 3 and, after completing his pilot training, sailed for England on October 14, arriving about three weeks before the Armistice ended the fighting on the Western Front.

In May 1918, an RAF recruiting office was set up in Saint John that then administered recruitment throughout the province. Captain Burpee Hay from Woodstock took charge of recruiting. By then, the twenty-seven-year-old veteran had accumulated a wealth of experience. During his time as a pilot, he flew BE.2A, 2B, and 2C aircraft and FE.2B and 2Cs. In May 1916, he became a flying officer with No. 25 Squadron and was seriously injured on July 17 when, while returning from a "nightly bombardment," he encountered fog and crashed his aircraft. According to the *Daily Telegraph*, the plane "turned turtle and fell on [Hay's] back," inflicting serious spinal injuries that left his legs "useless for a time." In September, he was sent to hospital in England and after being declared unfit for service was invalided back to Canada. After convalescing, Hay returned to duty and in November 1917 became the officer in charge of records and statistics at the headquarters of the recently formed Military District No. 7 in Saint John. In March 1918, Hay was sent back to France to take up ground duties with the RFC, but was again declared unfit for active service and returned to New Brunswick, where, in April, he became the RAF recruiting officer for the province.

In May 1918, Hay made a tour of the province, including Woodstock, Fredericton, and Moncton, looking for recruits. He also recruited in parts of Nova Scotia and Prince Edward Island. Within New Brunswick he was assisted by local recruiters such as J.J. McCaffery and Sergeant-Major H.T. Brewer in Fredericton and Captain Alex Creighton and W.H. Price in Moncton.

In June 1918, a renewed campaign for mechanics took place. The recruitment drive met with success, and late that month the intake of pilot cadets temporarily ceased except for those of the nineteen-year-old class under the Military Service Act, who were enlisted and placed on a reserve list. The temporary lull was necessary to allow the training schools time to process the large number of cadets already in hand. Nevertheless, the shortage of skilled and unskilled mechanics persisted, and recruiting standards were relaxed to include any men in the Class "B" medical category, as well as married men. Recruiters reminded prospective enlistees of the benefits of joining the RAF: the pay was good and promotion rapid; they were taught a trade that would be "invaluable to them after the war, since the field for aviation mechanics will be a large one"; and by joining the RAF, "a man is doing splendid work for his country in training pilots."

In late September, in order to speed up the process, the RAF centralized its recruiting in eastern Canada by having the Montreal office take over the districts then being administered by headquarters in Saint John and Halifax. Thereafter, recruits who passed a preliminary examination would go to Montreal for attestation en route to Toronto. To make sure prospective candidates throughout the Maritime region received up-to-date information, the system of local committees and sub-committees was extended. Recruitment of mechanics — who were "very apt to be overlooked in the glamor of the prospect of actual flying" — remained a priority. In its bid to do its "part nobly to make the world as free as its own element — the air," in the words of an article in the Daily Telegraph, the RAF's recruiting categories for cadets and mechanics now included men between the ages of eighteen and thirty of the Class "A" medical category and eighteen and 45 in Class "B." These recruiting efforts met with success, and large numbers of New Brunswickers enlisted in 1918 as flying cadets and mechanics. After completing their preliminary training in Canada, the former proceeded to England for their advanced training, while many of the latter served at local training schools.

Among the Canadian airmen who entered the RAF in the final stages of the war were those who joined the fledgling Canadian Air Force (CAF). In August 1918, a two-squadron wing of Canadians was authorized and attached to the RAF, but was slow to mobilize and never became operational. Heber John Cripps from Sussex joined their ground crew. Born on March 29, 1888, Cripps was a carpenter and builder before the war. On January 3, 1916, the thirty-four-year-old husband and father of two children enlisted in the 104th Battalion. After reaching England he was

Ground crew from Nos. 1 and 2 Squadrons, Canadian Air Force, Upper Heyford, England. LAC-3523046

transferred to the 13th Reserve Battalion. A newspaper article in the *Kings County Record* published in November 1918 described his efforts to join the British air services: "Corporal Cripps was turned down after reaching England as being medically unfit but afterward joined a Forestry Battalion and later a labor unit, but after reaching France was again turned down. However, he persisted in doing his bit and was accepted by the air forces of which he is now a member." On August 15, 1918, he was taken on command with the CAF Depot at Blandford, in England, and then, on November 20, shortly after the Armistice, joined No. 1 Squadron, CAF. As an Airman Mechanic 1st Class, he served initially as a carpenter and later as Aircraft Rigger 2nd Class. In July 1919, he returned to New Brunswick and was subsequently demobilized.

It is difficult to know how many New Brunswickers volunteered for the British air services, especially during the later stages of the war. The names of dozens of aspiring cadets and mechanics are found in local newspapers, especially during 1918, but some do not appear in official records as qualified airmen, suggesting they failed either to meet medical and other standards once they reached Toronto or to complete their instruction. Those recruits who successfully entered the ranks of the air services moved on to the next step in their bid to become active service airmen by undergoing training.

Chapter Two

Training Overseas and in Canada

Canadian airmen received their training in different places depending on where and when they joined the air services. Many of the early airmen who served initially in the CEF and transferred to the RFC or RNAS underwent their training in Britain and France. Later, after the RFC Canada training scheme was created in early 1917, airmen enlisting in Canada took their preliminary training at home in Ontario and, for a time, in Texas in the United States. Those who then moved on to Britain received their advanced training there. Some went on to become training instructors themselves, both in Britain and in Canada.

Early Training in Britain and France

The first step in training in Britain after candidates had transferred from the CEF to the air services was ground training. Insight into this phase can be learned through the experience of Lieutenant Charles Frederick Cawley. Unlike many of the well-educated provincial airmen who went on to become pilots, Cawley came from more humble beginnings. Born on July 23, 1893, in St. George, Charlotte County, Cawley's father, Frederick, was a builder. Following in his father's footsteps, Charles became a carpenter and worked as a builder and contractor from 1913 to 1915. He enlisted in the 115th Battalion on February 9, 1916, in Saint John at age twenty-two.

Bombing class at the RFC's No. 1 School of Military Aeronautics, Reading, England. An RE.7 light bomber and reconnaissance aircraft is seen in the background. MC 300/MS 69/23, PANB

After undergoing basic training at Valcartier, Cawley embarked from Halifax and sailed to Liverpool, arriving on July 31. Over the next several months, he served in different units and was eventually promoted to acting company sergeant major with the 6th Canadian Reserve Brigade at Bramshott, in Hampshire, serving as a bombing instructor.

On September 14, 1917, Cawley transferred to the RFC, and a few weeks later joined No. 1 Cadet Wing at Hastings, Sussex, where he began training. On January 23, 1918, he was commissioned and then joined No. 2 Training School at Northolt in west London for more advanced training. Through Cawley's training manuals and pilot's flying logbook held at the New Brunswick Museum, we get a good picture of the various phases of his introductory training. By early December, 1917, he was undergoing daily lectures and classes on a wide range of topics, including wireless telegraphy, map reading, the theory of flight, compass reading, Vickers machine guns, reconnaissance (observation and photography), instruments, engines — including pistons, connecting rods, the lubrication system, and carburetors — 112-lb bombs, the CFS (Central Flying School) bomb sight, the airplane control system and rigging, gunnery, including counterbattery fire, photography, cross-country flying, and contact patrols. The work was highly detailed and contained an incredible amount of information that had to be learned in a short period of time.

From there Cawley went on to flight training. On March 12, 1918, he made his first flight with an instructor in an airplane equipped with dual controls. The next day he took over the controls and made several turns and one landing, noting "feel OK." On May 11, he made his first solo flight, and then completed his long and comprehensive training during the week of August 8. He underwent instruction on several aircraft, including the Maurice Farman Shorthorn, an Avro trainer (likely the type S-11), and much more powerful fighter aircraft such as the Sopwith Pup and SE.5.

After receiving his Aero Club pilot's licence, Lloyd Sands from Moncton went to England, where he entered the RNAS on February 3, 1916, as a temporary flight sub-lieutenant. Shortly afterwards, he began flight training with the short course and progressed through the various phases. By May he had received four hours of dual instruction, but in June he "got only three landings one day, total time 25 minutes." By the time he went solo, he had received only four hours and fifty-nine minutes of dual instruction. In a letter home published in the *Moncton Daily Times*, he explained: "There were six of us in our class and I got the least dual instruction of any of them, not because I was clever but because, I think the instructor was fed up with me — I mean, I don't think he had any special love for me. However, on July 5th I got away solo. Since then had 2 hrs, 53 minutes solo flight putting in 1 hr., 37 minutes on July 5." During this time, he also received two weeks of instruction on motors in the aerodrome engine shop.

For Sands, solo flying consisted of trips over the aerodrome at about 2,000 feet and learning to land by shutting off the engine and heading the aircraft downward at 75 knots, or about 85 miles per hour (mph). He also practised right turns — "I'm poor at right turns." His flights lasted for up

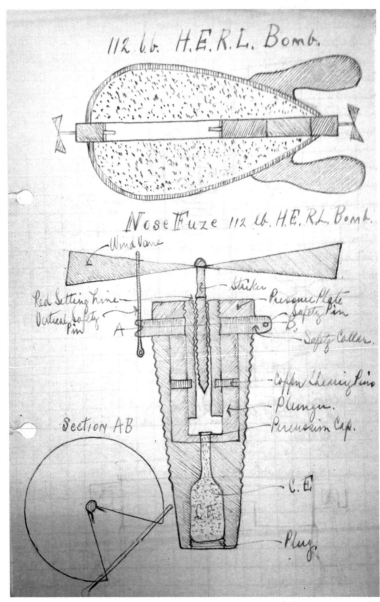

112 lb. H.E.R.L. Bomb.

Nose Fuze 112 lb. H.E.R.L. Bomb.

Wind Vane

Striker

Red Setting Line

Vertical Safety Pin

A

Pressure Plate

Safety Pin

B

Safety Collar

Coffin Shearing Pins

Plunger

Percussion Cap

Section AB

C.E.

Plug

Drawing of a 112-lb HERL (High Explosive, Royal Laboratories) bomb.
Cawley Collection, NBM

to 41 minutes and sometimes he flew to between 3,100 and 3,200 feet high. He wrote that solo flying "helped me a lot. I have more confidence and can judge things far better. I shut my engine off at 3,000 feet yesterday and glided into the aerodrome with an occasional 'blip'. (short 2 or 3 seconds of running) to keep up my speed."

Take-offs and landings were particularly dangerous. In September 1916, Sands described one of his adventures.

> I'm coming along with my flying. Have in over 18 hours, now, and have graduated from Caudrons on which I learned, and am flying solo on Blériots, Avros and Curtisses. The last named is some "bus." It can be flown level at a speed of 80 m.p.h. Some speed, eh? A short time ago [a Zeppelin] passed over here and dropped six bombs on the flying field and three on a race course next to the aerodrome, and thereby nearly got me into trouble, because the next day, in making my first landing solo, in a Curtiss, I hit just in front of a bomb crater—fifteen feet across—and bounced right over it. Good thing I didn't light in it. I'd have broken my neck and cost the Government a few thousand dollars for a new machine.

Alfred Belliveau began pilot training at Shoreham on large, two-seater Maurice Farman aircraft. In his memoir, he wrote: "They were very stable and easy to fly.... These planes were of the 'pusher' type with the motor and propellor behind the seats. The student sat in the front seat and the instructor in the back seat, with duplicate controls. The instructor also had a speaking tube leading to head phones at the student's position, thus emitting one-way communication." He added, somewhat tongue-in cheek, "It was said that the instructor also had a length of lead pipe available in his position to permit him to knock the student out if he froze at the controls. I would not know about that!"

Belliveau passed on to more advanced training at Dover Field on top of the White Cliffs near Dover harbour. By then, it was mid-winter and good flying days were scarce, and so progress was slow. Gradually, he

Lieutenant Alfred Belliveau in front of a
Sopwith Camel at Dover airfield, England, 1917.

P37-B021, Centre d'études acadiennes Anselme-Chiasson, Université de Moncton

accumulated flying time on two-seater Avros with an instructor and then moved on to Sopwith Pup and Sopwith Camel single-seaters. According to Belliveau, "the Avros were a very stable plane and a pleasure to fly, but the Pups and Camels were tricky." He related that on his first flight in a Camel his Australian instructor came close to the side of the plane and said: "Belliveau, when you take off, be damn sure to fly *straight ahead* till you get up to 4,000 feet. And don't try any kind of a turn until you get there. She's hell on a right turn." Beliveau touched his helmet and said, "Yes, Sir!" When he reached 4,000 feet he tried a sharp right turn. "And sure enough, I fell into a tight spin, straight down, due to the heavy torque this light plane developed. And it was also reputed to be difficult to pull out of a spin. But I got it out all right, with the aid of a steep dive, and then went on to make a few more right turns till I got the knack. Then I tried some more maneuvers including a few landings."

Once he graduated on the Camel, he went to the top finishing school for fighter pilots at Turnberry, Scotland, on the site of the famous golf course. There he practised stunt flying over and over, and firing at stationary targets on the ground and at aerial targets being towed through the air by another plane over the water. "We also did a lot of 'dog fighting' in man to man aerial combat, but using cameras in place of machine guns, the cameras being synchronized with the propellor blades like the machine guns were, so as to enable us to take pictures of our opponent through the whirling propellors in the same manner as in actual combat with machine guns."

Among the other airmen from New Brunswick who undertook their training in Britain was Weldon Carter. Born in Saint John in May 1896, Carter moved to Fredericton, where he attended UNB between 1913 and 1916. On September 15, 1916, he joined the 1st Canadian Garrison Artillery Regiment in Halifax as a lieutenant. Then, in early February 1917, he reverted to the ranks and enlisted as a gunner in the CEF's 76th Depot Battery, Canadian Field Artillery (CFA) at Winnipeg. On July 5, he arrived in England as a sergeant in a siege battery draft and served with the artillery until transferring to the RNAS in mid-October. He was ordered to report to ground school at Greenwich, near London, for preliminary training. There, he joined about three hundred probationary flight officers to receive instruction in meteorology, wireless telegraphy, the theory of flight, engines, gunnery, aerial navigation, and foot drill.

After about eight weeks, Carter went to the aerodrome at Eastbourne, Sussex, for flight training—what he called "real" flying. He had mixed feelings about his first flight. On the one hand, "the sensations one experiences when in the air for the first time are rather disappointing —one expects to have one's heart in one's mouth at all times but as a matter of fact unless it is a 'bumpy' day there is very little more motion to an aeroplane than to a small boat when a choppy sea is running." Nevertheless, he never forgot his first flight. "The pilot, who was afterwards my instructor showed me how to get in the machine. He then handed me a peculiar looking helmet with a long rubber tube attached to it and told me to put it on. Then he got in the machine behind me himself. At the word 'Contact' the propellor was given a sharp turn and the engine roared—soon its roar became a gentle purr." The telephone helmets enabled the student and instructor to speak to each other. The pilot instructed him to "fasten your belt and never go up in future without seeing that you are well strapped in."

They waited for at least five minutes for the engine to warm up before the throttle could be opened wide. Carter pushed his feet forward onto the rudder bar and gripped the "joy" stick between his legs. The pilot told him always to take off and land directly into the wind. During the take-off, "it seemed to me that I was going faster than I had ever before, and I readily confess that I did not like it as we left the ground. Soon I overcame the desire to keep my head well down in the machine and I looked over the side. Just then the machine gave a lurch and I drew in my head with a jerk."

It took time for him to get used to the sense of movement, especially at higher altitudes. "The country below was like a map on a very large scale, but it seemed to me after we had reached a very considerable height, that we were stationary and that the map was moving. ... It took several flights before I could get rid of this illusion." During the flight, the pilot did a "stunt," putting the aircraft into a stall.

The engine was throttled down and the nose pointed toward the earth in a fairly steep dive. As soon as we had reached a good speed the nose pointed towards the sky — up — up — up — we seemed to go — then we seemed to lose speed and soon it appeared that we were hanging in mid-air. That was an awful sensation. Suddenly the nose of the machine fairly snapped down and it seemed that we were doomed to dive straight into the ground. Right here I want to say that I "had the wind up." Soon we were flying on the level again and I heaved a sigh of relief.

Carter also vividly described his first solo flight.

No pilot can deny that during his first solo he was very much frightened. I was no exception to the rule. However, I got off the ground fairly well and started left hand circuits of the aerodrome. Strange thoughts of engine failure assailed my mind and I was in constant dread of colliding with other machines. After I thought I had been up for an hour (although I had scarcely been up fifteen minutes) I decided to land. I had just "flattened out" and was waiting for my wheels to touch the ground when — crash — I had landed right on top of another machine in the middle of the drome. Both machines were wrecks, although fortunately the pilot of the other machine and I were both unhurt.

After a few more solos, Carter tried stunts: loops, rolls, spins, and Immelmann turns. "Stunting while of little or no use in war flying, is greatly encouraged because it tends to increase a pupil's confidence in his machine."

With about twenty hours of soloing, Carter went to Cranwell aerodrome in Lincolnshire in early February 1918 for advanced training on active service aircraft. There he flew "scouts" — small, single-seater fighters that required more skill to fly. They included Bristol Bullets and Pups — his favourite plane, which was "light on controls and easy to land." Then he moved on to Camels — "a very tricky machine to fly," being prone to spins. But once mastered it was "a great old 'bus.' Many a time later on, its quickness to answer controls was responsible for my escaping with a whole skin." After some firing in the air and practise in formation flying, Carter was appointed an active service pilot with the rank of flight sub-lieutenant, and in May proceeded to France. Once he arrived and was assigned to an active service squadron, he still had much to learn. Carter made it his policy "to talk shop to the experienced pilots as much as possible." He observed that most pilots who were killed died within a month of arriving while they were still learning their craft.

Bristol Bullet. MC 300/MS 69/23, PANB

The Experience of Flying

Carter's observations were not uncommon: for most of these airmen, flying was a new experience that left a vivid impression on them. Lieutenant Raymond Haley of Saint John, an observer with the RFC's No. 9 Squadron, described his experience during a test flight in October 1917 in a high-performance aircraft, published in the *St. Croix Courier*.

I had quite an experience yesterday flying with one of our crack pilots, Wadham, famous here for his spins. He asked for an observer, as he wanted to go up and test his engines. We took off against a strong wind, and just after leaving the ground he made a sharp turn to the right and banked so steeply that he appeared to put one wing tip on the ground and described a quarter of a circle. Then he flew along level to within about 30 feet of a row of trees and put the nose straight up. Finally we gained about 2,000 feet and came down steeply to within 20 feet of the ground — the engine full on going about 110 miles per hour and turned sharply just missing a hangar. Then we climbed up to about 500 feet and put the machine into a spin. It was certainly the funniest sensation of all in flying. From the ground the machine looks absolutely out of control — nose vertical downwards and the whole machine revolving rapidly. We went around about 20 times, then came out at 300 feet, and side slipped on to the aerodrome. From the plane in a spin the ground seems to be turning around at an awful rate, and the machine in the opposite direction so that one gets very dizzy.

Later, as they improved and became more sophisticated, airmen wrote about the increasing performance of their aircraft. In September 1918, Lieutenant George Boyer from Hartland, newly arrived in England as an instructor, in a letter to his mother printed in the *Carleton Observer*, described the thrill of flying a state-of-the-art Sopwith Snipe.

I was flying a new machine today, a machine that has just come out. They call it a Snipe. It has a spread of wings only 12-feet from tip to tip, but it is all motor; a nine cylinder rotary motor, 200 horse power, with a speed of 200 miles per hour and a wonderful machine to fly. I am not sorry now that I did not stay in Canada as an instructor, because I am flying machines that will get Huns if any will. They will climb at an angle of 45 degrees, at 90 miles per hour, and will go absolutely straight up 500 feet. They are a wonderful machine and I am proud to be able to fly one of them. They carry 2 guns that shoot 1,000 shots per minute.

Sopwith Snipe. MC 300/MS 69/23, PANB

Training in Canada

Once the RFC/RAF Canada scheme was established at home, newly attested airmen received their preliminary training at the several camps set up in Ontario and during the winter of 1917/18 in Texas. Those destined for overseas service underwent advanced training once they reached Britain. Like training for airmen recruited in Britain, cadets in Canada began with ground training, consisting of a few weeks at the depot, where recruits were introduced to military life through drill and physical fitness training and basic instruction on military discipline. From there they went to the Cadet Wing at Long Branch for eight weeks of physical conditioning and introductory lectures in flying basics, including aerial navigation, wireless usage, and signalling. Then they joined the School of Military

Classroom instruction at the RFC Canada School of Aeronautics, University of Toronto. LAC C-0200396

Aeronautics at the University of Toronto for a month, where they learned about the theory of flight, meteorology, engines, artillery observation, bombs, and machine guns.

The next phase was basic flight training at camps at Long Branch, Borden, and Deseronto, consisting of dual instruction and solo flying, followed by more advanced training at Borden in formation flying, bombing, artillery observation, and aerial machine gunnery. Once this phase was completed, the cadets became qualified pilots and were ready to move on to active service training in Britain, where they received a more advanced short course in flying, commonly known as "stunts," and flew newer types of aircraft preparatory to being posted to operational squadrons at the front.

Among the early New Brunswick cadets to receive their advanced training in Britain was Lieutenant Leonard Atwood Richardson, who was born in Richardson, on Deer Island in Charlotte County, studied engineering at Acadia University in Wolfville, Nova Scotia, and then moved to the Massachusetts Institute of Technology in Boston. In early July 1917, he travelled to Toronto, where he became a flying cadet in the RFC a month before his twenty-third birthday. For his preliminary training, he took a course at the School of Military Aeronautics. According to his diary, published as *Pilot's Log*, half the students were Americans, three-quarters of them "university men." They did drill and studied aeronautics and wireless. In August, he went to Camp Mohawk at Deseronto for flight training on the JN-4D ("Jenny"). He had seven hours of dual flying instruction and then ten and a half hours of solo flying experience, during which he had no crashes and made sixty successful landings. From there he went to Camp Borden for a finishing course consisting of wireless shoots, cross-country flying, and aerobatics.

Mechanics also received physical fitness instruction and a short course in military discipline at the outset of their training, and then more focused instruction in their chosen trades. A lengthy article appearing in the *Daily Gleaner* in June 1917 colourfully described the scope of their training.

> They begin with theory, lectures before a blackboard on any one of a hundred things, then practical work on engines, and the parts of engines, magnetos and similar mysteries, the splicing of wire and the making of joints which will resist sudden strains, the turning of steel, the intricacies of tool making and the finer points of the cabinet makers' art.... Even upholstering and the working of leather is to be taught, for My Lord the fighting man, for whose delectation all this work is being done must sit in comfort upon an aluminum chair with seat and back softened by curled hair.

During the winter of 1917/18, when inclement weather interrupted training in Ontario, many RFC cadets and mechanics from New Brunswick went to Camp Taliaferro at Fort Worth, Texas, for training. Among the mechanics was Wellington Austin Smith from Saint John, who was a motor cyclist and chauffeur before enlisting in the RFC scheme

Trainer JN-4C. LAC C-3623081

in Toronto on October 20, 1917. During his time in Texas, he was promoted to air mechanic 2nd class, which gave him a pay raise of twenty-five cents a day. However, he had his problems during his time there. In a letter to his grandmother dated February 1, 1918, held at the Provincial Archives of New Brunswick, he recounted how he had been "layed [*sic*] up for some time with a broken wrist. Was starting one of the planes and got hit with the propellor and broke my wrist but am lucky at that as it might have broken my neck. Lots of the boys have broken arms in the same way and quite a few have lost their lives but I am worth a dozen dead men yet." He was also being quarantined with measles, sleeping in a tent with three others: "All we have to do is sleep, read, and smoke, and keep the fire going." He concluded by writing that "we are expecting to move back to Toronto sometime in March and believe me March can't get here any too quick for me as I am getting pretty sick of Texas."

The Dangerous Nature of Flight Training

Flight training was dangerous work, and many accidents and several deaths in Canada and Texas were the result. Novice pilots frequently crashed during practice landings. Mechanical failures with their machines and adverse weather conditions also made training hazardous for air crew. In August 1917, Kenneth Foster McFarlane of Nashwaaksis enlisted in the RFC in Toronto and underwent training to become an observer. On December 24, during his instruction at Camp Leaside, he was seriously injured. By then, he'd been up several times with his pilot for a total of twenty-three hours. When at about 7,000 feet, they hit an air pocket. In a newspaper report in the *Saint John Globe*, McFarlane explained that, "when a machine strikes an air pocket, there is no air for the propellor to get hold of, and it just drops. Their machine dropped 7,000 feet. When it struck the air it was with such force that it snapped one of the controlling planes, and the machine became unmanageable. It pitched head first to the ground, crashing onto a shell factory. It all happened so quickly they didn't know what had taken place." The pilot died of his injuries two days later and McFarlane's right leg and arm were broken, which kept him in hospital until April.

Several of the fatalities among the province's airmen came as a result of flying accidents during training, both at home and overseas. On April 29, 1918, Cadet Edgar LeBlanc from Moncton was killed at Camp Mohawk. In a letter to LeBlanc's mother published in the *Moncton Daily Times*, Captain J. Lloyd Williams from No. 81 Canadian Training Squadron described the accident.

He had been with me for five weeks and was nearly ready to go solo. At the time of the accident he was under instruction with my senior instructor and they were seen to be coming down in a spin which is part of the usual course of instruction. Like most aeroplane accidents little more can be found out because the instructor is seriously injured and not expected to recover. It is doubly hard to have a relation or friend killed before getting on to the battle front, but with us, unlike other branches of the service the risk to a small degree starts with the commencement of training. Your son's kit has been packed and sent to the officer in charge of records, who will send the same along to you. The cause of death of your son was fractured skull and all we could do for him was done, the ambulance being on the scene of the crash within a few minutes. Again expressing the sincere sympathy of all who knew your son.

Another airman killed during training was Joseph Daniel Brosnan, who died in Texas. Born in Saint John, before the war Brosnan was an accountant with T.B. and H.R. Robinson, insurance brokers, and was active in the Knights of Columbus as their treasurer, the St. Peter's Church Young Men's Association, and Young Men's Christian Institute. He enlisted in the RFC on November 9, 1917, along with several other Saint Johners who went to Toronto for preliminary training. After spending Christmas with his parents, he returned to Toronto and then went to Camp Taliaferro in Texas for more training. In a letter to his parents printed in the *Saint John Globe*, he wrote that he had been in the air on the same day as fellow New Brunswick cadet, Guy Scovil from Saint John, and mentioned cadets Frederick Power and J.B. Patterson, both from Saint John.

On February 9, 1918, Brosnan died in a training accident while flying a Curtiss Jenny at Benbrook Field, part of the Camp Taliaferro complex. According to fellow cadet Fred Power, Joseph's closest friend in the training squadron, he was "making his first flight alone with a stiff breeze blowing. He was given the word and started his engine. When he was about 300 feet in the air it was seen that something was wrong and soon the aeroplane plunged to earth. It was thought by those about that the cadet had lost control of the machine and thus the end came. The young man was dead, a doctor said, when he struck the ground." The meaning of the doctor's statement is not clear; whether it was meant to comfort the family or suggested Bronsan had some kind of physical attack. According to Power, Joseph's "sunny ways and genial good cheer had endeared him to all." To remember his friend, Power had a cane made from the wreckage

Gravestone of Cadet Joseph D. Brosnan, St. Joseph's Roman Catholic Cemetery, Saint John. Author's photo

of the aircraft. Brosnan's body was repatriated for burial in Saint John at St. Joseph's Roman Catholic Cemetery.

Fatal accidents also occurred among New Brunswick airmen while training in Britain. They included Second Lieutenant Charles Hedley Edgecombe of Fredericton. Born on July 16, 1888, Charles was the eldest son of F.B. Edgecombe, who owned F.B. Edgecombe and Company Limited, a large dry goods business in Fredericton, where Charles worked from 1908 to 1917. According to his RAF service file, by the time Charles enlisted he had a knowledge of motor cars and motorboats. In November 1917, he became a cadet in the RFC Canada scheme and underwent training in Toronto and Texas. He was appointed a temporary second lieutenant on July 25, 1918. According to the *Saint John Globe*, he was assigned to be an instructor, "but revolted at this work, much preferring to get into active service." He received a leave of absence until August 15, when he reported for overseas service. When he sailed from Quebec in charge of a company of twenty-five other aviators, his father was there to say goodbye. On September 11, he joined No. 42 Wing of the RAF's Home Establishment, and then on the twenty-eighth transferred to No. 11 Training Division Station (TDS) at Old Sarum, Salisbury, for ten days of instruction before being assigned to a "bombing machine." He made two trial flights with a qualified pilot, the second of which proved fatal on October 6. While news of the accident was received by family on October 8, details of his death were not disclosed until December 9, when a letter from a fellow aviator, Captain D. Stewart Shepherd, was printed in the *Daily Gleaner*.

Dear Sir:

...the late Lieut. Edgecombe went as a passenger with 2nd Lieutenant Forster on a cross country flight on the 6th October flying in the observer seat of a DH.9. Second Lt. Forster was qualified to carry a passenger. He had a forced landing, nothing serious was wrong. About 3 o'clock the following day the machine was ready to start again. The machine took off all right and climbed to 300 or 400 feet when 2nd Lieut. Forster made a steep left turn. The wind was gusty and appeared to get under the machine and turn it over, and it spun into the ground. It burst into flames, and by the time assistance arrived Lieut. Edgecombe was beyond help. Second Lieut. Forster was badly injured and died the same evening. Lieut. Edgecombe's body was buried with full air force honors at Salisbury.

Advanced Training in Britain for Canadian Airmen

By June 1917, the first draft of cadet pilots trained in Canada sailed to Britain to undergo the next step in their preparation for active service. The experiences of Lieutenant Leonard Richardson aptly illustrate this final transition. After graduating from the RFC Canada program in October, Richardson went on leave in New York, where his family then lived, and in mid-November he boarded the SS *Megantic* at Montreal with sixty RFC officers for the trip to England. Upon arriving at Liverpool, Richardson proceeded to London and, after reporting to RFC headquarters, took several days' leave. He was nonetheless keen to get to his flight training camp: "Well, I will be glad to get out to the Squadron and back to work, as London is getting tiresome, especially as we have nothing to do but kill time."

The first stage of Richardson's advanced training took place from December 15, 1917, to February 1, 1918, with No. 93 Squadron at Camp Challis Hill, near Stockbridge, Hampshire. During his first day in the air on the eighteenth flying an Avro 504K, the same aircraft he flew at Borden, he practised spins and landings many times with an instructor.

It was cut short by engine troubles. The next day he flew solo. He found the Avro was better than the Jenny, being "nicer to handle." On December 22, he began flying "stunts," such as loops, spins, and Immelmann turns, which Richardson called "split-assing." During the day's training he got lost and had to make a forced landing, and then swing his own propellor to get going again. Next, he made a cross-country flight to Gosport, Southampton, and Plymouth — "a fine sight" — and the English Channel. However, the fumes from the castor oil engine lubricant gave him a "beastly headache" and so he "washed out" after lunch.

Training in the winter months was difficult when high winds, rain, snow, and mist kept him grounded on many days. On December 28, Richardson lamented: "We seem to make little progress." In the cold weather, the pilot's flying kit consisted of fur-lined gloves and goggles, and a flying coat.

On January 1, 1918, Richardson flew a Sopwith Pup for the first time. "Pups are nice little busses to handle." But these flimsy aircraft had their limits. A week later, he was flying a Pup in windy conditions and after landing was taxiing to the hangar "perhaps a little too fast, when a gust of wind caught the 'Pup' and turned it over on its back. Two mechanics came out, righted the machine and I continued to the hangar." On another windy day a few weeks later he again "busted a 'Pup' taxiing in; the wind lifted the thing and turned it on its back. I hung upside down until some guy pulled me out."

On February 1, he began the next leg of his advanced training when he went to the No. 1 School of Aerial Fighting and Gunnery at Turnberry, Scotland. Headquarters was in a stately two-hundred-room hotel at the famous golf course, complete with a fine mess and laundry service. Amid the beautiful setting, he walked the beach picking up seashells, which reminded him of Deer Island. "I must say I am greatly impressed."

In many ways the training was not very different from what he received at Borden, but among the new practices was ground machine gunnery, where he shot on ranges at balloons with tracers from an old BE.2c — "it is great sport." Overall, however, Richardson had a low opinion of the training. The ground gunnery course he called "a joke compared to Borden. It certainly isn't much practice for France."

On February 13, he passed his tests and moved north about twenty-five miles to Ayr for the final round of advanced training in combat aircraft. Carleton House, a large old house, served as their barracks. It was "very nice but lacking furniture. However, we are comfortable, and the mess is great." The aerodrome was located two miles away, and a London double-decker bus was used to "cart us back and forth." There, he was assigned to a Sopwith Camel squadron initially and then to SE.5s, which he much preferred. His instructors were "top fighters on home leave from France."

Constant rain kept them from flying for some time. When they did begin practising, he again used an Avro 504K, flying dual at 140 mph on the level and 210 mph in a dive, practising stunting and fighting. On February 26, while sitting in an Avro, another flier taxied into him and "smashed both machines." In March, summery weather prevailed, and he got in more practice fighting and formation flying in SE.5s, and he soon soloed. He was impressed with the SE.5: "Oh Boy! Lord they have power and what a wonderful feeling to have that long nose out in front."

On March 3, Richardson reluctantly left Ayr and reported to headquarters in London for assignment to an overseas squadron. The next day he left for the RNAS War School at Camp Manston in eastern Kent to begin his final round of advanced training. Manston was the largest aerodrome he'd ever seen: "miles and miles, perfectly flat." He visited the hangars, where he saw DH.4s and DH.9s, and air raid shelters forty feet deep. The mess and sleeping quarters were on the base and the "gun room" was available for playing cards and writing.

Much to his disappointment, his "finish" training was on Sopwith Camels. He began training flying a Pup, practising stunts and fighting, and then quickly soloed on a Camel. "Camels are the most damnable busses ever. Sitting way out on the nose in a dirty 'Office' [cockpit] blinded by wings, you aviate through the atmosphere, wherever the old bus wishes to take you." In frustration he wrote: "I am disgusted with the way my R.F.C. career is turning out. If I have to go to France on a 'Camel' I will be forced to say HELL." Over the next several days he continued flying Camels over the River Thames, where he "popped off" ammunition and saw many ships out in the Channel.

On March 12, he left Manston for the base at London Colney, where he was posted to No. 74 Overseas Squadron for training on SE.5s. Despite many "dud" days due to poor weather, he soloed on an SE.5 even though he had only forty-five minutes on them. On March 22, his advanced training finally ended when Richardson and his squadron moved to France.

When the Armistice took effect in November, many flight cadets from the RAF Canada scheme were still undergoing training or were waiting to take their final examinations in Canada. In early December, they were sent home on two months' provisional discharge. At the same time, a large number of New Brunswickers who joined the air services in 1918 and completed their introductory training in Canada were still undergoing advanced training in Britain or awaiting assignment to operational squadrons when the war ended. Among the latter was Kenneth Colin Irving. Born in Bouctouche in Kent County on March 14, 1899, his father James ran a prosperous lumber business and general store. After the war

began, Kenneth tried to enlist when he was still in high school, but his father refused to give his consent. Another attempt while he was a student at Dalhousie University and member of the Canadian Officers' Training Corps (COTC) was similarly

Second Lieutenant Kenneth C. Irving.
Courtesy of Harold Wright

thwarted. He finally got his wish when he joined the RAF Canada scheme in Toronto on May 15, 1918. After undergoing elementary cadet pilot training, he graduated on September 19 and embarked for England, where he joined the cadet wing of the RAF on October 5. During his advanced pilot training, one of his instructors was his cousin and boyhood friend, Leigh Stevenson. Three months after the Armistice, his training ended and on February 15, 1919, he received the rank of 2nd Lieutenant Overseas Cadet. On April 11, Irving was sent to Shorncliffe for repatriation back to Canada.

Instructors

Successful training depended on the instructors provided by the air services, both in Britain and Canada. Several New Brunswickers became training instructors once they were commissioned. Among them was Flight Lieutenant George A. Boyer of Hartland. Before enlisting, he was an Inspector of Munitions at the International Steel and Ordnance Company in Lowell, Massachusetts. According to an article printed in the *Carleton Observer* in December 1918, he enlisted in the RFC in October 1917 as a motor driver. "He made good at this and his natural quickness and steady nerve won the attention of officers in the flying service and he was transferred to that section." During the winter of 1917/18, he underwent flight training in Texas and was involved in three crashes. "The third one proved quite disastrous, for when after 24 hours he recovered conscious [*sic*] it was to realize he had a leg broken below the knee and his hip injured." He remained in hospital for four months, "and it was feared his flying nerve might have departed."

> His Captain told him if he desired to remain in the flying section he would have to submit to a severe test for nerve. He readily agreed, and was told to climb to as high an altitude as his machine would take him, then to throw out all controls and plunge aimlessly through the air until he reached 500 feet from the ground then to right his machine and land safely. Lieutenant Boyer performed his feat and is still in the service.

In August 1918, while at Toronto, Boyer was one of five chosen from among fifty candidates to become a flight lieutenant and instructor. In September, he left for England and was posted to a camp at Hounslow Heath in Middlesex. He continued as an instructor until the end of the war. While serving with the RFC/RAF, he accumulated 31 hours and 20 minutes of solo flying.

Another instructor was Lieutenant Walter H. Irvine, who was born in Chicago on October 1, 1897, the son of Dr. Walter J. Irvine, and grew up in St. Mary's across the Saint John River from Fredericton. According to newspaper articles, he was well suited for becoming a military instructor. The *Daily Gleaner* reported:

> From the time he was fourteen years of age, he took a deep interest in all things of a military nature and took as naturally to the soldier's life as a duck does to water. In the High School he was active in the Cadet Corps. During his High School days he attended the encampments at Sussex. He became proficient in military tactics in all its branches. During these years he received from Sir Sam Hughes a 1st Class Rifleman's Certificate, also the Lord Strathcona medal for sharpshooting, and a certificate for signalling.

After graduating from high school, the seventeen-year-old Irvine enlisted on October 25, 1915, in the 104th Battalion at Sussex as a private and was later promoted to sergeant. On June 28, 1916, he sailed from Halifax to England with the 104th aboard the *Olympic*. According to the *Daily Gleaner*, "he showed he had the faculty of imparting his knowledge," and became a sergeant instructor in physical, bayonet, and machine-gun drill. "He was ambitious for the aviation work, but was held back from this on the advice of superior officers, as his services were needed in other lines." Nevertheless, on November 10, 1917, Sergeant Irvine was taken on command with the RFC at St. Leonards-on-Sea, in Sussex.

On January 23, 1918, Irvine was commissioned as a lieutenant in the RFC, and soon became an aviation instructor. According to a June 1918 article in the *Saint John Globe*, "he had the rare gift of imparting the knowledge he had acquired so that others could grasp the idea and, under his tutelage, develop it.... To take fellows into the clouds, show them how to duck, glide, side-step and hand out the count is now his work."

Yet another instructor was Leigh Forbes Stevenson. Born on May 24, 1895, in Richibucto, Stevenson became a bank clerk and served for five years in the New Brunswick militia's 73rd Northumberland Regiment. In 1911, he moved to Roblin, Manitoba, with his widowed mother, Mary, where he worked as a bank clerk with the Union Bank of Canada. On December 23, 1914, he began a lengthy and varied service with the CEF when he enlisted as a private in the 32nd Battalion in Winnipeg. On February 23, 1915, he sailed to England, and on March 15 was promoted to sergeant. Then, in early May, he was transferred to the 8th Battalion in France, where he served until late April 1916, whereupon he re-crossed the Channel to England and then returned to Canada to take up a commission. He was attached to an officers' training course at the Royal School of

Infantry in Halifax, and in September Lieutenant Stevenson joined the 145th Battalion (New Brunswick), raised in the southeastern section of the province. Then, in January 1917, he was taken on strength with the 236th Battalion (The New Brunswick Kilties) in Fredericton. In November, he returned to Britain, where the disbanded Kilties were absorbed into the

Lieutenant Leigh F. Stevenson.
Courtesy of Harold Wright

20th Reserve Battalion. On March 23, 1918, Stevenson was attached to the RFC and underwent flight training at Reading. On September 1, he became an assistant instructor and later instructor at No. 54 Training Depot Station. In February 1919, he was repatriated to Canada.

Some also served as instructors at home, including Lieutenant John Edward Hanning from Fredericton, who was posted to Canada on June 30, 1918, after extensive experience at the front. He served as an instructor at No. 4 School of Aeronautics at the University of Toronto for the rest of his service. Another veteran airman was Captain Wilfred Landry, who was born on November 10, 1888, in Dorchester, and was educated at the Collège Saint-Joseph at nearby Memramcook. He served in the militia's 19th Battery, stationed in Moncton. From 1905 to 1910, he attended McGill University in Montreal, and became an electrical engineer in the west. Early in the war, the twenty-seven-year-old Landry returned to New Brunswick and took the somewhat unconventional route of enlisting as a gunner in the 23rd Battery, 6th Brigade, CFA in early December 1914. After drilling for a few months, he transferred to Kingston, Ontario, where he attended an artillery course and qualified as a lieutenant in February 1915. In July, he joined the 17th Battery, CFA, then being mobilized at Camp Sewell near Winnipeg, as a lieutenant. Shortly afterwards, the unit sailed for England and then fought at the front, where Landry was promoted to captain. He was transferred to Headquarters, RFC on August 27, 1916, and then seconded to air crew as an observer on October 11. After returning home in October 1917 from active service in France as an observer and pilot, he became an instructor at No. 89 Canadian Training Squadron at a training camp in Ontario.

It took months of training both at home and overseas for New Brunswick's airmen to become fully qualified pilots, observers, and mechanics. For many, the next step was to join front-line British air services squadrons in France and Belgium and begin active operations against the Germans.

Chapter Three

Operations on the Western Front

As the use of aircraft during the Great War became more diverse, airmen engaged in several combat roles in the fighting on the Western Front in Belgium and France. Beginning with reconnaissance, of both land and sea, they soon also undertook fighter operations against enemy aircraft, and then close ground support for the infantry and bombing raids behind the front lines and deep into Germany. New Brunswickers were present during all these missions.

Reconnaissance

Early in the war, the air services' main role was reconnaissance, working with the artillery as spotters and conducting aerial photography. These remained critical missions throughout the fighting. In the forefront of these operations were the observers who relayed information to the gunners using wireless, took aerial photographs, and acted as air gunners using Lewis machine guns to provide protection from enemy attacks. Several provincial observers wrote detailed accounts of their experiences.

Among New Brunswick's early RFC observers was Lieutenant Lee Roy Brown, who was born on March 6, 1890, at Westmorland Point. On January 5, 1915, he enlisted in the Canadian Army Service Corps in Winnipeg, and went overseas in early September. In August 1916, he was

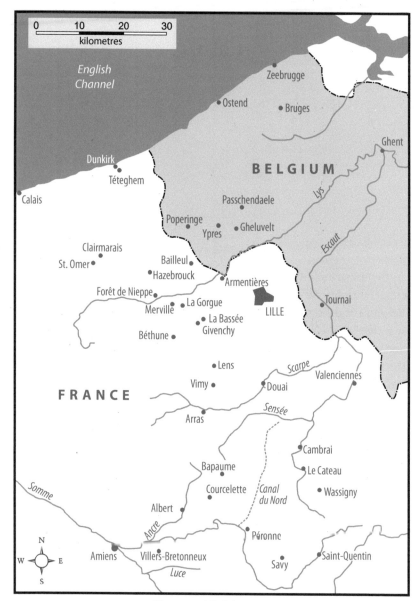

France and Belgium. MB

attached to the RFC, was appointed a second lieutenant in October, and joined No. 15 Squadron on November 21. He wrote a letter to his mother that was printed in the *Moncton Daily Times* in March 1917 in which he vividly describes the novelty of his first combat mission as an observer. "I could hardly sleep that night at all for thinking of the fact that one of my greatest ambitions was about to be realized and wondering what it would be like and how I would be affected by my first trip in the air." At 5:30 a.m. the next day, he donned his leather flying clothes, climbed into the aircraft being flown by his flight commander, took off, and headed toward the front lines.

Of course, I had some difficulty in finding out my location. I had my maps with me and finally after a lot of looking located a large town over which Captain S----[his flight commander] told me he would circle a few times so that I would know where I was. There was also a long straight road which crossed the firing line at nearly right angles, which I was told would be a very good guide for me. By this time we had climbed to nearly 6000 feet. I had no difficulty in finding the road but was rather puzzled by finding that shortly after leaving the large town...the road disappeared altogether to appear again some distance further ahead. As I was trying to puzzle out what was the reason that the road was not kept up for this distance we were passing over the missing part and rapidly nearing where it commenced again. I also noticed that the ground looked rather pitted and rough and was wondering what caused it to look that way when suddenly I was awakened by a tremendous "krump" seemingly right in my ear. The machine immediately canted over in an angle of nearly 90 degrees, righted itself and swung over nearly as far the other way. Of course I was tossed about and between hanging in and recovering my wits I had a very busy time of it. (I never want to get such a start again as long as I live.) I think for a moment I would have taken a nickle and given up all my prospects of flying. I could not begin to tell you all of the thoughts that ran through my head that second. (Ha, ha.)

He continued his account.

> When I finally recovered enough to look around I noticed a
> large puff of black smoke right where the machine would have
> been if the pilot had not so suddenly (without consulting me if
> you please) altered its course. Remember all of this happened in
> less than a second. I was very much surprised to find that the
> machine was intact and that neither the pilot nor I was killed.
> The sound of the first shell had hardly died away when four or
> five more followed one another in rapid succession, but I was
> prepared for anything so did not get such a rude jar as the first
> one gave me. The air was soon full of puffs of smoke and we beat
> it back to our own lines where I felt much safer.... When we got
> back to our lines the engine began missing badly and we were
> forced to come back to the aerodrome after an hour full of very
> novel and exciting experiences. On examining the machine we
> found that only two pieces of shell had hit it and in places that
> did not affect the running of it in any way.

They changed into another plane, took off immediately, and flew a less
eventful mission. "I landed at ten after a very exciting four and a half hours
ready for breakfast and keen for another try at any time. I did not feel a bit
sick or uncomfortable in any way. I rather expected to be a bit seasick on
my first trip as beginners usually suffer in that way."

Brown was wounded in March 1917 and after returning to active duty
undertook pilot training. On April 5, 1918, he joined No. 57 Squadron
and began carrying out reconnaissance missions, including a dangerous
flight that earned him the Distinguished Flying Cross (DFC). According
to the citation:

> On the 25th June 1918, whilst on counter-battery photography
> near Courcelette this officer was attacked by two Triplanes and
> four Biplanes. Lieutenant Brown's gravity tank exploded and
> caught fire but blew out. His centre section struts were shot

through, also his wind screen and altogether there were 50 holes in his machine. After about one-quarter hour's fighting in which he was forced down from 18,000 to 8,000 feet he found he had reached over the lines and the enemy aircraft left him. He then climbed to 19,000 feet and returned to complete his photography, making a further 24 exposures.

His pluck and determination in resuming his photography after having been so badly shot about is a splendid example to the rest of the squadron.

In an article in the *St. Croix Courier*, Lieutenant Raymond Robins Haley of Saint John also described one of his reconnaissance missions as an observer with the RFC's No. 9 Squadron in October 1917, in which his aircraft came under attack and was badly damaged, and he engaged in his role as an air gunner.

I was in a rather bad affair early yesterday morning on "flash patrol," which means cruising up and down just behind our lines watching for Hun batteries to flash, sending down calls on the wireless and getting our batteries going on them. I went up at 5:45 [p.m.] with a new pilot. The sun was very bad, shining in our eyes so that we could scarcely see anything on the ground. We had only about fifteen minutes to complete our three mile tour when we were suddenly attacked by five Albatross scouts in formation. Only three came after us, the other two stayed above for protection. The scrap lasted two or three minutes, but seemed like ten. They each took turns diving and firing, and at each I got off a good burst which kept them off. All the time my pilot kept his nerve and kept zigzagging to put them off their shot. While I was changing drums, one got in a good burst and I felt the machine lurch to one side and thought the pilot was hit, but I soon had my second drum going and they all turned tail for the Hun lines, and I gave them a farewell burst just to let them know we were still in fighting trim. Then I turned around to see if the pilot was hit and found to my joy that he was all right; but the poor old machine was a sad cripple, the pilot had the control lever in the left hand corner, holding it there with both knees and both hands. I looked around and found that our aileron control had been shot away on one side, which gave us a right bank, so that even with the control lever away to the left were still sideslipping and had a list of about 20 degrees. I was contemplating getting out on the left wing to balance it. I found that four or five wires had been shot way. Also a bullet had gone through the wind screen and must have passed about two inches from both our heads.

He continued his description of the mission.

After hours, it seemed, we reached the aerodrome and had to make a flat turn for fear of getting in a spin. Eventually, we made rather a good landing, but when we touched the ground you could feel everything give way. The engine had been hit, too, and gave a final cough and stopped just as we reached the ground. There were twenty holes through the machine, two through the propeller, several through the fuselage and, in fact, the machine was a wreck, and we can't yet understand how we got back. The bullets had passed all around us, but we were not hit. I must have been rather lucky with some of my shots, or they wouldn't have cleared off so quickly. In all I fired 200 rounds with my machine gun, so I hope some of them found a mark. It was some scrap.

Another observer was Lieutenant Wilfred Landry. Between August 28, 1916, and February 15, 1917, Landry served with No. 42 Squadron at the front, a reconnaissance unit that flew BE.2s and carried out artillery observation and tactical reconnaissance. On his third mission, Landry and his English pilot, Second Lieutenant H. Jameson, were sent to help bring down a German observation balloon. The following narrative is drawn from their combat report.

At 3.25 p.m. on 21-9-16 we left the ground carrying two Lewis guns, two 20 lb bombs and six drums of ammunition, for the purpose of escorting 2/Lt Dunckley, who was carrying out an attack on the Hostile Kite Balloon.... After attaining a height of 7,000 feet we took up a position on the right of the bombing machine. Both machines then proceeded towards Armentieres. On reaching Armentieres we flew in an S.E. direction through the clouds for a period of 8 to 10 minutes. Judging we were in the neighborhood of our objective we dived through the clouds with the object of joining up with the bombing machine. As soon as we came out of the clouds at a height of 5,000 feet we saw the balloon being pulled down 2 or 3 miles away. During this time we came under a heavy fire from A.A. guns. One shell exploded just in front of the machine, making an 8" hole in the side of the front petrol tank. The tank quickly emptied, drenching the pilot and observer with petrol. This being the tank the machine was running on, the engine stopped. The pilot at once switched on to the back tank, but on finding the engine would not pick up, he decided to do as much damage to the balloon as possible before landing, as we were now out of gliding distance of our lines. At a height of 1,000 feet the two 20-lb bombs were dropped on the balloon, which was by this time on the ground. Both bombs were seen to explode close to the target but no damage was observed. When we got down to a height of 600 to 700 feet the pilot fired a drum of Buckingham Tracers at the balloon. He then maneouvred [sic] the machine so as to enable the observer to fire. The observer, [Landry] who was standing on the seat, emptied two drums at the balloon, and some seemed to ricochet off the envelope. A team of 6 or 8 horses were near the balloon, having no doubt been used to haul it down. While firing one of these horses was observed to fall. All the men near the balloon seemed to be either running away or firing with rifles. During this time we came under a heavy rifle and machine gun fire from a village 3 or 400 yards away. Immediately the engine picked up we started

"The Young Man's Element," by Frederick H. Varley. The sketch shows an observer firing his Lewis machine gun. CWM 19710261-0777

to make for our own lines. As we left the vicinity of the balloon both the pilot and observer fired into the neighboring villages for the purposes of keeping down the enemy's fire. Crossing the trenches at 1,300 feet, the machine was subjected to a very heavy rifle and machine gun fire, but as no vital parts were hit, we were able to land safely in our own aerodrome. The envelope of the balloon attacked was yellow and had three black crosses painted on it. It did not appear to be fully inflated.

On February 15, 1917, while the squadron was stationed at Bailleul, near the Belgian border, Landry was injured when his aircraft's engine failed and the plane fell about 400 feet and crashed through the roof of a building. The pilot received a serious head injury, while Landry was dazed but never lost consciousness, and suffered a dislocated nose and damaged chin. He was hospitalized in France and London until he was discharged on February 26.

In the spring of 1917, upon recovering, Landry, like Lee Roy Brown, underwent training as a pilot and received his wings in June. The next month he joined No. 75 (Home Defence) Squadron in eastern England, where he flew a BE.2 scout aircraft until late September, when he returned to Canada to become an instructor with a training squadron. He was later mentioned for valuable service in connection with the war.

Finally, observation was also carried out by air officers from balloons. Among them was Lieutenant John Harper Evans from Moncton, who was a civil engineer living in Woodstock when the war began and had six years' experience with the 19th Battery, CFA. Early in the war, he joined the CEF with the 19th and went overseas, where he saw action during the Second Battle of Ypres. On September 25, 1915, he was attached to the Royal Navy's Kite Balloon Section and became an air observer, using tethered or captured hydrogen balloons that ascended to over 2,500 feet. According to a report in the *Moncton Daily Times*, he accompanied "the artillery making several ascents over the enemy's lines at daybreak and reported back at once to the artillery commanders the position of the enemy so that their fire might be effective."

In mid-November, Evans returned to the Canadian Training Division at Shorncliffe, was attached to the Home Establishment of the RFC, and sent to the RNAS school at Roehampton for further training, where he made several balloon ascents. On December 18, he went up with three other trainees to 6,000 feet, above the clouds, when he was involved in a serious accident. According to the account in the *Daily Times*,

> They had been in the air 1 hour and 10 minutes and had travelled about 56 miles. They decided to descend but let out a little too much gas and immediately began to fall. To avoid this they threw out all of their ballast, but the balloon continued to descend. Up above, the air was quite calm, but down below a 40-mile wind was blowing which changed the course of the balloon and caused it to crash into the side of a hill. Then as soon

as the basket rested on the ground and the weight was taken off the balloon immediately shot up again, rising to a height of about 3,000 feet and carrying the occupants of the car with it. When the car crashed into the ground, Lieut. Evans was rendered unconscious and had his ankle broken. When the balloon reached the height of 3,000 feet it began gradually to descend but no further harm resulted.

After the accident Evans was sent to Queen Alexandra Hospital in London, where he was confined for about eight weeks for treatment of a sprained ankle. Unfortunately, he did not complete his training but was transferred back to the CEF and, in February 1916, returned to Canada on leave. He eventually took command of the 65th Field Battery in Woodstock and returned to France, where he served for the rest of the war, eventually rising to the rank of major.

Fighter Pilots

As the struggle for air supremacy continued, fighter or scout pilots flew combat patrols aimed at keeping the Germans at bay and allowing the reconnaissance aircraft to get on with their work in relative safety. By April 1917, Flight Sub-Lieutenant Lloyd Sands was stationed at Dunkirk, the RNAS's main base on the English Channel, from which they flew most of their offensive operations against the Germans. In July, Sands was credited with driving down two enemy aircraft out of control.

New Brunswick's Alfred Belliveau also joined the ranks of fighter pilots. On June 8, 1918, he was ordered to report to the pilots' pool at Saint-Omer in France, which he did by flying across the Channel in a brand-new Sopwith Camel scout. He then joined No. 54 Squadron at Boisdinghem, to the west of Saint-Omer, and became one of eight pilots in C Flight, which consisted of three Englishmen, three Canadians, a South African, and an American.

They moved frequently along the front once the Allies took the offensive beginning in the summer of 1918. On June 30, the squadron travelled to Estrée-Blanche, northwest of Béthune, and then on July 4–5

Lieutenant Alfred Belliveau in the cockpit of his Sopwith Camel.
P37-B022, Centre d'études acadiennes Anselme-Chiasson, Université de Moncton

to Vignacourt, north of Amiens. On July 14, they moved to Touquin, thirty miles southeast of Paris, to take part in the American attacks at Château-Thierry and Saint-Mihiel. After this they shifted north again, arriving later in August at Avesnes, near the Channel coast southeast of Boulogne. An account in Sydney F. Wise's *Canadian Airmen* describes Belliveau's participation in combat with enemy planes:

> On August 22 [1918] . . . four Sopwith Camels of 54 Squadron, led by Captain E.J. Salter of Mimico, Ont., and including Lieutenants A.H. Belliveau of Fredericton and A.S. Compton of Toronto, met a patrol of four enemy aircraft coming west from Bapaume. The German machines were obviously flown by inexperienced pilots. Despite having the sun in their eyes, Salter's flight apparently saw their enemy first and were able

to manoeuvre themselves into a position above and behind the Germans. They then dived in line-ahead formation on the highest of the enemy machines, a two-seater Albatross, and each of them gave it a short burst in turn. The Albatross went into a nose-dive and was seen to crash.

Belliveau also carried out attacks against enemy artillery observation balloons well behind the German lines that were calling down fire on British artillery positions. The aircraft used incendiary Buckingham ammunition that set the balloons on fire.

In 1917, Captain Albert Desbrisay Carter became New Brunswick's pre-eminent Great War "ace." He was born at Point de Bute, Westmorland County, near the Nova Scotia border, on July 3, 1892, the only son of Leonard and Violetta "Ettie" (Goodwin) Carter. He studied at Stanstead College, a private boarding school in Quebec, and in 1914, when the war broke out, he was a twenty-two-year-old student at Mount Allison University in Sackville. He had served in the 74th Regiment (The New Brunswick Rangers) of the provincial militia for three years, having been commissioned as a lieutenant on April 18, 1912, and becoming a cadet instructor. In November 1914, "Nick"—as his friends called him—joined the 26th New Brunswick Battalion as a lieutenant. According to the *Moncton Daily Times*, "he was given a rousing send-off by the students of Mount Allison and a suitable gift was handed him before leaving." Carter became a company commander until the unit was reorganized, whereupon he was appointed its machine-gun officer. He went overseas with the battalion in June 1915 and then to France on September 15, where he was seriously wounded in the right hip and thigh during the 26th's first major action, the Battle of the Crater, on October 13. He was hospitalized in Britain for some time and never returned to the 26th. He came home to New Brunswick in mid-November to convalesce.

By then, it is likely that Carter had already become interested in flying. In an interview with a *Daily Telegraph* reporter shortly after returning home, he recounted how a German plane manoeuvring over the 26th's

Major Albert Desbrisay Carter.
2007.07/1656, Mount Allison University Archives

trenches was brought down. The pilot survived but was badly wounded, and then injured in the fall. By a strange coincidence, when Carter was admitted to hospital after being wounded, he recognized in the bed beside him the German pilot who "fell from the clouds." He spoke with him in English, but the German airman was reserved and would not talk about the war or conditions at home except to admit that "things could be better." Carter also talked about airplane duels that went on overhead constantly. Sometimes several of the Germans would concentrate at a point, drop bombs, and then return to their own lines. He also related: "I saw a Zeppelin raid over Dover. There was a good deal of damage done but the military damage was nothing of importance."

On June 19, 1916, Carter joined the 140th Battalion at Saint John, one of several infantry battalions raised within the province in 1915–16, and was promoted to major and command of "A" Company. In September, he returned overseas with the 140th. Captain Dugald Stuart Bell from Saint John, a fellow officer in the battalion, confirmed Carter's growing interest in flying in an article in the *St. John Standard* published in May 1919. "When he reached England we were for a time at Shoreham and both Carter and myself enjoyed the privilege of going up in the air. Carter remarked when he came down from his first flight, 'I will never be satisfied until I get into the Royal Flying Corps.'"

After the 140th was broken up for reinforcements, Carter was briefly on strength with the Princess Patricia's Canadian Light Infantry, The Royal Canadian Regiment, and then the 13th New Brunswick Reserve Battalion. On May 26, 1917, Carter got his wish when he was detached to the RFC at Reading and underwent pilot training on a range of aircraft with various training squadrons until mid-September. On August 14, he was appointed a flying officer and seconded to the RFC with the rank of major. By the end of September, he had arrived at Bailleul, in France, where he joined "B" Flight of No. 19 Squadron, a fighter squadron that flew SPAD VII aircraft.

The squadron carried out two main roles: offensive patrols against enemy aircraft and ground support operations. In the first case, it encountered German *Jastas* (squadrons) that mostly flew Albatross scouts; in the second, it supported Canadian and British troops during the later stages of the Third Ypres campaign around Passchendaele, strafing German troops.

Carter got his first two victories on October 31 near Gheluvelt, east of Ypres. He described his first engagement with a German C-Type machine in his combat report.

> I dived on three EA [enemy aircraft] and picking out one dived vertically on to it. I came to within about ten yards of it and had to pull out in order not to crash. I fired many bursts into the pilot's and observer's seats, starting from 150 yards until I had to pull out. I am certain I got the EA as the bullets seemed to pour into the pilot's and observer's cockpit and finally the observer stopped firing. I could not see what happened to the EA when we got near the ground; I finished off considerably under 1000 ft. If AA confirms that this machine was out of control it must have crashed.

A British anti-aircraft battery confirmed the attack, and Carter was awarded his first official victory.

Carter accounted for another fourteen enemy aircraft over the next two months, mostly Albatross scouts. He also carried out strafing operations

Sopwith Dolphin fighter. LAC-3390997

around Passchendaele, against both German horse and mechanical transport and their trenches, often in adverse weather conditions. He was promoted to officer commanding "B" Flight on November 14, by which time he had four victories. Others soon followed, including two more downed aircraft — a Pfalz DIII and an Albatross — on December 18, the latter with assistance from Captain Frank Ormond Soden, commander of "C" Flight from No. 60 Squadron, who had been born in Petitcodiac and moved to England as a youth.

By mid-November, No. 19 Squadron had received a prototype of the new Sopwith Dolphin fighter for evaluation, and on December 28 the first front-line Dolphins arrived. Throughout early 1918, the squadron was withdrawn from active operations as it made the transition to the new fighter, which had greater firepower with two fixed, synchronized Vickers guns and an upper-wing-mounted Lewis gun. It was also fitted with racks for dropping bombs. Its 200-horsepower engine ensured greater power, especially at higher altitudes.

After returning from leave, Carter got his first victory with a Dolphin on March 12, near Menin. He also used the plane to drop bombs on

German troops, especially those moving on roads in massed formations. A report stated that, on March 27, during the great German offensive south of Arras, "Major Carter dropped four bombs on German infantry which was seen marching along the Bapaume-Albert Road and afterwards he traversed another portion of the same road several times firing into troops (which were in close formation) from 900 ft. and completely scattering the German formations. A total of 300 rounds were fired by the pilot."

On March 31, the squadron moved southeast to Savy to begin operations providing cover for No. 18 Squadron's DH.4 day bombers that were being used for long-range reconnaissance. By mid-May, Carter's victories had increased to twenty-eight enemy aircraft and he had distinguished himself as a fighter pilot. In mid-December 1916, he was recommended by his commanding officer for promotion to squadron commander, "as he is an officer of exceptional character. He is a first-rate pilot, and exceedingly keen and skillful pilot and is very conscientious." He was decorated with several prestigious awards for his service, including the Distinguished Service Order (DSO) and Bar and the Belgian Croix de Guerre, and was also mentioned in despatches.

Carter's successes were widely reported in New Brunswick newspapers. In early March 1918, the *Moncton Daily Times* noted that he "is winning fame as an aviator. He is not only daring, but eminently successful." Later, after he went missing, the *Daily Telegraph* stated that "New Brunswick has produced no more daring and gallant officer during the present war than 'Nick' Carter."

On May 19, 1918, Carter was shot down behind enemy lines near La Bassée, captured, and spent the rest of the war in German prisoner-of-war (POW) camps until being repatriated to Britain at the end of the war.

Day-to-Day Operations

Lieutenant Leonard Richardson's diary and letters offer a detailed picture of daily life with No. 74 Squadron during active operations at the front between late March and mid-July 1918. After a couple of false starts, he landed at Calais on March 29 and started his way "up the line" via Dunkirk to nearby Téteghem, the site of No. 74's aerodrome. Among the squadron's veteran fliers was Captain Edward C. "Mick" Mannock, "A" Flight's commander, who already had forty victories. As Richardson wrote, "I am sure I could not have gotten a better squadron."

As the squadron's spare pilot, Richardson got little airtime initially; instead, he carried out other duties, including travelling by car to Saint-Omer, site of the RFC's headquarters, to pick up stores, such as extra struts, and sometimes staying overnight in a hotel. To pass the time, he played football in the afternoons and sat by the fire reading and playing cards in the evenings.

The squadron had arrived during the German offensive in Flanders. "We can hear the Bosch artillery articulating. We know not the wherefore but it appears the front is fluid and getting a bit closer to us." On April 9, they got orders to move, and initially shifted to Poperinghe, where they came under German fire, and then two days later moved to Clairmarais, just outside Saint-Omer. According to Richardson, "It is a damn rotten hole. Not much of a landing field." The officers lived in wooden huts, two to a hut. The mess was in another wooden hut and the hangars were made from canvas.

Operational squadrons consisted of eighteen aircraft organized into three, six-plane flights. By early 1918, when carrying out routine flying, they did three patrols of two flights each per day. Typically, "A" and "B" Flights did an early morning ("dawn") patrol, "A" and "C" Flights flew at noon, and "B" and "C" in the late afternoon. Each patrol flew up to two hours, which was the petrol limit for most aircraft. Occasionally, they flew a full squadron "show" in the evening. A flight's typical flying formation had three aircraft side by side, including the flight leader, two above them, and the sixth plane above everyone. When diving to attack, they would close up on the flight leader and follow him down. Typically, they carried out one of several types of missions: bombing, strafing, or line flights, where they flew along a line on the map patrolling for enemy aircraft. Occasionally, they also escorted other squadrons on larger-scale bombing missions.

On April 23, Richardson made his first sortie over the Forêt de Nieppe, near Bailleul, during which he saw five German Albatross fighters but "no excitement." On the twenty-seventh, he flew to Bailleul and Armentières on a bombing run. Although they had no contact with enemy aircraft, when he was about twenty miles behind enemy lines they got "Archied" by German anti-aircraft guns at about 4,000 feet. As he told his mother in a letter, they dropped their "eggs" and started "split-assing about for all we were worth, banks, dives, climbs and all sorts of comic stunts: that's the way we dodge Archie. Then we got machine gun bullets; tracers and field pieces have at us. Believe me. I sure had 'wind up' but we got through alright." He continued: "Flying low, bombing and strafing is a rotten game.... Well, I'm getting used to the game, but believe me, I sure didn't feel at home the first few times." In his diary he recorded sardonically: "It's a Hell of a game. Someone will eventually get hurt."

At the end of April, he received a new SE.5. "She's a peach; gives 110 miles across the carpet at 1,800 feet." It was quickly initiated. On May 1, he made a one-and-a-quarter-hour flight to Merville carrying out a line patrol. They met no enemy aircraft, but were hit again by anti-aircraft fire near Bailleul and the Forêt de Nieppe. The lower right plane of his "bus" had the fabric stripped off, and a burst of machine-gun bullets that passed through the fuselage "just past my nose, scares the Hell out of me. Headed for home with machine more or less shot up. Got lost but got back." Then, on May 2 he crash-landed when he hit a bump, breaking the V-strut and wing, which had to be repaired. The next day he carried out a high-level bombing raid at Kemmel, south of Ypres, but when the plane's throttle seized, he had to head for home. The effects of these bombing operations could be quite spectacular. On June 2, during an attack near Bac Saint-Maur, southwest of Armentières, "Glory be," Richardson recounted, "what a colossal explosion we created. Every machine feels it at 14,000 feet. I thought I was hit. It was a cracker."

Throughout much of May 1918, the squadron carried out patrols almost every day. On the seventeenth, "B" and "C" Flights flew a dawn patrol over La Gorgue and Merville at 14,000 feet ("upstairs"). Richardson's description offers a vivid picture of "dog fighting."

We get in one hell of a dog fight with 10 Pfalz [single-seat scouts] from the Jagdsaffeln [German squadron]. I shoot up two, hit one, but there are so many machines everywhere that we almost shoot each other. We dove on them from above and as the SE is a better machine we can usually zoom out of the dive and stay above the enemy but these damn Pfalz have a habit of sideslipping underneath as we dive on them. Unless the enemy are "en flamme," it is impossible to watch them go down and therefore confirmation is contingent on some other source. Nixon goes down in flames on his first flight over. I nearly collide with Mick [Mannock] in the scrap; I was zooming up while he was diving and I thought for a minute we had had it. Mick said after that he thought our wings scraped. Another scrape like that and I will have a heart attack.

On May 19, the squadron dropped bombs, strafed trenches, and "chased around a bit" near Comines. Richardson was in awe of Mannock's skills. "Mick gets another Hun in flames and out of control. I don't know how he does it. He just picks them out of the air." On the same day, Mannock was awarded the DSO and on May 30 the Bar to his DSO.

Richardson became frustrated by his inability to score a victory. On May 21, when Mannock got his forty-fourth "kill," he wrote: "I certainly wish I could get one or two. I've been in nearly every scrap that 'C' flight has had, I get in the shooting as early as Cairns [his flight leader] does but either I'm a darn rotten shot or my Huns that I have shot up are out of control and one can't take the time to watch to see if they crash." On May 30, his frustration became more acute: "I pooped at two but didn't seem to do much harm and they were in my ring sight. I just don't know what's wrong with me unless it is the damn glasses I have to wear under my goggles. I do go into all the scraps and I do shoot at the damn Huns and that must at least annoy them? But I can't seem to connect." In time he came to accept his bad luck. In a letter to his mother on June 7, he wrote: "been in about 8 fights and although I didn't get official credit I am satisfied that I sent at least 1 down."

Combat pilots had to live with the changeable fortunes of operations. On May 8, Richardson experienced "A Hellish day for #74 Squadron" when they lost four pilots, including one whose wings let go over the drome and he dove into the runway and went up in flames. "Such a terrible sight. We pick up his remains in a bushel basket and will give him a military funeral. He was a Canadian and a damn swell boy." Richardson wrote a poem in his memory.

R.I.P.

No pomp or splendour followed him,
To his resting place out there.
No Silver casket or flowered Urn,
Or Bishop grand to say a prayer.
The Padre man and his comrades,
In their service Khaki dressed,
Offered a prayer, their past respect,
Then lay him away to rest.
Wrapped in the flag he served,
We wait that short reprieve,
Side by side with a hundred more,
He sleeps, and yet we grieve.
No token for memory is needed,
Yet at his head stands a cross.
His was the life of profit,
Ours, the life of loss.

The next day one of the missing pilots returned; he had landed his plane near the German lines, burned it, and then crossed over to the British front lines, where he spent the night. Four days later, the squadron had "damnable good luck; we even up the score with Fritz," when they shot down seven enemy planes. Three were brought down by Mannock. "He just banked from one to another in seconds. He is a terrific leader. He moves around in the air in such a way that the Hun doesn't know where he is or what he has in mind—sometimes we don't either until we find the flight in a diving position with enemy in front and below." Mannock was posted as commanding officer of No. 85 Squadron in June and was killed in action on July 26, 1918. He was awarded the VC (posthumously), DSO and two Bars, and MC and Bar, and amassed sixty-one victories.

Not every mission was furious action. During patrols when no contact occurred, some pilots went sightseeing. On June 3, Richardson and two others flew south to Arras, where Nos. 64 and 19 Squadrons were stationed. "Saw no one but lots of scenery.... Beautiful country down south, rolling hills, green, etc. #64 has a beautiful situation." The next day, with no enemy planes around, he flew up the coast "to see the water and a long strip of sand beach that runs from Dunkirk to Ostend." Dawn patrols also offered spectacular sights. On June 10, Richardson rose at 3:10 a.m. and left when it was still dark. "We keep formation by watching the flames from the exhaust pipes of the other machines. By the time we climb to 10,000 feet it is getting light and the sun is appearing over the horizon in the East; it is the sight of a lifetime, too wonderful to describe. It is something you feel."

Close Ground Support Operations

As time went on, the air services took on new roles. Some airmen became involved in ground support operations where they assisted infantry during attacks. According to Weldon Carter, "it consists of flying low over the enemy territory, dropping bombs on any good targets and using machine guns on his trenches and transport." He also pointed out that the "casualties during this kind of work are heavy, but it must have a very telling effect on the enemy's morale. I can imagine nothing more terrifying than to look up to find an aeroplane roaring down on one with both machine guns spitting tracer bullets."

On September 27, 1918, Carter was flying ground support sorties with No. 201 Squadron during the Allied attack on the Canal du Nord. According to a letter dated September 28 that was printed in the University of New Brunswick's *Monthly Magazine* in November 1918,

our squadron was doing low flying, shooting up Hun troops. (This is the worst job we have to do.) I had done some very nice work among the blue uniforms with my guns and bombs when phat! I was hit in the engine and my petrol pipe shot away, and I was nicely over Hun land with very little height to glide west to our lines. The ground was a honey-comb of shell holes and fresh ones were appearing faster than I could count them — a lovely place for a forced landing — don't you think. So I saw that I must crash and believe me I did one peach. My machine was matchwood and I was on my head in the very middle of our barrage, just ahead of our tanks. I got out of my bus (or rather its wreckage) and started west, and you can take it from me it would have been a smart Hun that caught me. It's lucky my middle name is "Speedy."

Along the way Carter found a wounded British Tommy (infantryman) whom he carried on his shoulder until he got two German prisoners to carry the soldier back to the British lines. Before departing, one of the prisoners gave Carter his Iron Cross, First Class, "saying in broken English that he would rather give it to me than have somebody pinch it from him." He eventually arrived at a British artillery battery, where he got a glass of whiskey, hopped on a lorry, and eventually arrived back at his aerodrome ten hours later. During his trek across No Man's Land, he had gathered several souvenirs, including two German revolvers, a pair of field glasses, three bayonets and belts, and a flashlight, all of which he had "decked about my person" when he arrived. He concluded by writing, "this as a great war, but I'd rather be in the air than on the ground after yesterday."

Bombing Operations

Other fliers became involved in medium- and long-range bomber operations that developed in the second half of the war. Initially, bombing was carried out by units of the RNAS and later the RAF from bases at Dunkirk. They included No. 218 Squadron, part of a day bomber wing that launched raids against the German-occupied ports of Bruges and Zeebrugge in Belgium. Among their pilots was Lieutenant (François) Frank Gallant from Rogersville in Northumberland County. Born on

April 14, 1899, Gallant was a student at St. Thomas College in Chatham from September 1909 to June 1914. When he enlisted in the 165th (Acadian) Battalion in Moncton on February 19, 1916, he gave his age as seventeen; in fact, he was still only sixteen. He proceeded to England with the battalion in March 1917, and when the unit was disbanded, he joined the Canadian Forestry Corps in early May. On January 19, 1918, he transferred to the RFC, underwent training, and then joined No. 218 Squadron on July 21, 1918, at age nineteen.

Airco DH.4 light day bomber. WikiCommons

Captain Michael Lawrence Doyle became a reconnaissance-bomber pilot. Born in River Louison in Restigouche County on November 26, 1889, he lived in Nash Creek and worked at the Royal Bank of Canada in nearby Jacquet River until moving to Montreal, where he continued to work for the bank until May 1915. He served with the militia's 55th Irish Canadian Rangers and spent nine months at the Spirit Lake Detention camp in northern Quebec doing garrison duty. On February 23, 1916, he joined the 199th Battalion, CEF, in Montreal as a captain, sailed to

England in mid-December, and after spending several months with various reserve and depot units, he was attached to the RFC on June 26, 1917, for training. He became a flying officer on November 27, and on February 25, 1918, he arrived in France and joined No. 25 Squadron, where he carried out numerous bombing and strafing missions flying a DH.4 against various targets during the German Spring Offensive in March. Between May 2 and November 17, 1918, he served with No. 42 Squadron, a reconnaissance-bomber unit that also flew DH.4 aircraft. On August 20, 1918, he received the DFC for gallantry and determination. His citation described some of his accomplishments.

On 8 August 1918 Captain Doyle successfully carried out three bomb raids on the Somme bridges from very low altitudes, although attacked by numerous enemy aircraft, machine gun and trench mortar fire from the ground. On 9 August 1918 he again carried out two low bomb raids. In addition, he was continuously engaged on low work during the first battle of Amiens in March and in May and July with the French on the Noyons-Montdidier-Chateau Thierry front, on all occasions displaying great gallantry and initiative. On 10 May 1918 he shot down two enemy aircraft in flames near Peronne, when attacked on a bomb raid by 30 enemy aircraft. Again on 6 June 1918, when over Monte Notre Dame he shot down an enemy aircraft completely out of control.

This officer has completed 40 bomb raids, 20 low bomb and ground raids, 6 photographic reconnaissances, making a total of 66 distinct flights, 29 of which he had led with conspicuous success. He has always shown great gallantry, judgement and foresight and has set a magnificent example to the pilots and observers in his squadron.

In June 1918, the RAF created the Independent Force to extend attacks against German positions as part of the British strategic bomber offensive. Among the New Brunswickers who joined the bombing operations was Flying Officer Donald Angus MacDonald. Born in Saint John on October

19, 1897, MacDonald graduated from UNB's forestry program in 1914 and became a forest engineer with the Dominion Forest Service, working as assistant supervisor of the Bow River Forestry Reserve in Alberta. Before the war, he served for a year and a half as a lieutenant in the 4th Forest Troop of the Canadian Engineers. On June 19, 1917, he enlisted at Ottawa as a lieutenant in the Canadian Forestry Corps, went overseas, and served with the corps' Base Depot in England. On September 19, he was seconded to the RFC, and after completing his training on February 12, 1918, was appointed flying officer. On April 25, he arrived in France for duty with the RAF's No. 99 Squadron, a day-bombing unit formed at Yatesbury, Wiltshire, the previous August. On May 3, they joined VIII Brigade, where they completed their training and familiarization. The squadron included ten Canadians, about a quarter of their strength, MacDonald among them. Equipped with Airco DH.9 bombers — new, longer-range day bombers that proved to be underpowered and prone to breakdowns over time — they began operations on May 24, when fourteen aircraft set off to bomb the Thyssenkrupp blast furnaces at Hagendingen, in the Moselle River valley north of Metz. Six of the aircraft were piloted by Canadians, including MacDonald. Eight planes reached the target and carried out their mission despite being attacked by several German Albatross scouts. Three days later, they suffered their first loss when MacDonald's plane was shot down behind German lines and he became a prisoner of war.

Lieutenant John Warren Price was an observer in a bomber squadron. He was born in Petitcodiac on January 25, 1892, to Margaret (Parker) and Claude Price, a terminal agent. When war came, he was working in Moncton as a commission merchant, with five years' service with the 19th Field Battery, CFA. In November 1914, he volunteered for service in the artillery in the Second Canadian Contingent, and was placed in charge of recruiting for the artillery in Moncton. He served briefly with No. 7 Siege Battery, but could not go overseas with them due to an injury. In November 1915, he joined the 9th Siege Battery in Saint John, becoming officer commanding No. 1 Section. He went to England in command of a draft for the battery, and on April 16, 1917, joined the RFC at Reading.

On June 1, 1917, he was attached to No. 100 Squadron, based at Izel-lès-Hameau, near Arras, as an observer on bombing raids into Germany in FE.2b night bombers. By early 1918, he had been deep into enemy territory at least thirty-five times, mostly at night. Price was quoted in a letter written by a London nurse, Anne Merrill, that was reprinted in the *Moncton Daily Times* in January 1918 in which he described the glorious moonlit nights when they could see their bombs bursting and the fires they started. "But it's the most awful sensation to be caught in the search-lights. You feel as though the whole world was looking at you. You feel as though you were about ump-teen times bigger than you are."

Maritime Operations

Members of the RNAS and later the RAF also carried out operations in support of the Royal Navy's war at sea and coastal patrols. John Blair Balfour Patterson from Saint John was a nineteen-year-old bank clerk when he joined the RFC Canada scheme in Toronto on November 13, 1917. After arriving in Britain, he made daily flights in a DH.6 aircraft hunting German submarines off the east coast of England between Hartlepool and Scarborough. Similarly, Royden Foley from Saint John enlisted in the RFC Canada scheme in early November 1917, underwent training in Ontario and Texas, and sailed overseas in April 1918, later joining No. 251 Squadron flying anti-submarine patrols off the Yorkshire coast in DH.6s, working with submarine chasers and convoying ships through the danger zone.

Second Lieutenant William Stanley Lockhart of Moncton provided ship protection at sea under quite extraordinary circumstances. Lockhart did his first two years of an electrical engineering degree at Mount Allison University, and then completed it at McGill University in Montreal. Afterwards, he moved to the United States, where he practised his profession for several years. He enlisted in the RFC in the fall of 1917. In time, Lockhart served on board the Australian light cruiser HMAS *Sydney*, flying a Sopwith Camel that took off from a gun turret platform. Needless to say, this was a challenging operation involving the ship's commander coordinating with the bridge, a midshipman taking the wind pressure, the pilot, and his aircraft mechanic. According to Wise's *Canadian Airmen*:

> When the aircraft, attached to the deck by cables ending in a quick release shackle, was in flying position the pilot and mechanic got the engine turning over. It was important to warm up the engine thoroughly despite the frequent impatience of the captain; otherwise the pilot might find himself moving down his twelve-foot runway with the engine barely ticking over. Once the engine was warm and the rpms and oil pressure in order, it was necessary to be dead into the wind, with at least twenty knots of wind pressure.

Lockhart recalled the operation in much detail:

> I always figured if 20 knots would take you off, 24 knots…would take you off better. The Snotty [midshipman] reports to the Commander an 18 knot wind pressure. The Commander says to me, "18 knots." I answer, "The ship will have to steam ahead 6 knots more." He says "How do you want your platform trained?" I say, "3 points green"…The bridge is right behind me and up about 8 feet, but I can't talk to the bridge. The Commander tells the bridge to steam ahead 6 knots faster and train the platform 3 points green. You feel the ship going ahead and the platform moves to starboard. Then the Snotty reports to the Commander "24 knots." I nod O.K. to the Commander, I try my ailerons, I try my rudder, my oil pressure is all right, my RPM is all right. I set my stick a little forward. I want to nose down a little to start with. I hold everything as is. I raise my left hand high. The Commander raises his white flag and my mechanic is watching him under the fuselage. I drop my hand back into the cockpit. The Commander lowers his flag. Birch [his mechanic] sees the signal and he pulls the trip cord. For the next two seconds you

don't know what has happened but you soon discover you are out there flying an aeroplane.

The next phase of the operation was landing. Since they were sometimes too far from terra firma, putting down at sea was often necessary. Landing on board a makeshift aircraft carrier was dangerous and avoided, and so they often ditched in the sea alongside the closest destroyer and were lifted out of the water.

Although most New Brunswick airmen fought on the Western Front against the Germans, others served further afield in the Mediterranean theatre fighting more distant enemies, including the Ottoman Turks and Bulgarians. Some also flew against the Germans in Russia and later still against the Bolsheviks. A few saw action long after the war on the Western Front ended in November 1918.

Chapter Four

Service on Other War Fronts

Although most Canadian airmen served on the Western Front, many others fought in the war's more distant theatres of operation, including Italy, Egypt, and Macedonia around the Mediterranean region, as well as in northern and southern Russia. The exploits of several New Brunswickers in these faraway campaigns were closely followed by provincial newspapers and their readers.

Italy

The Italian theatre was Britain's largest air commitment outside France and Belgium. At least two New Brunswickers served there with the air services. The earliest was Lieutenant George Egerton Stuart McLeod, who was born in Saint John on January 12, 1895. From 1910 to 1914, he attended Trinity College School, an independent boarding school in Port Hope, Ontario, and then was a student from January to December 1915 at the Royal Military College at Kingston. Afterwards, McLeod joined the Canadian Army Service Corps as a lieutenant and served for two years in horse transport and supply work. On November 15, 1917, he joined the RNAS and, beginning in early December, underwent training at Greenwich, Vendôme, in France, and Calshot Naval Air Station on the Hampshire coast. On May 29, 1918, he was appointed a second lieutenant

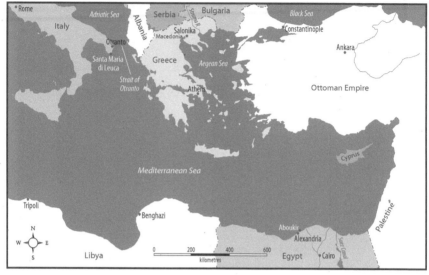

The Mediterranean Theatre of Operations. MB

and subsequently joined the RAF's Adriatic Group No. 10 as an observer at the seaplane station at Santa Maria di Leuca, south of Otranto, Italy. According to his air service file, he later graduated to become a seaplane pilot.

The group's task was to protect maritime routes through the Mediterranean in support of military operations in Italy, Macedonia, and Palestine against Austro-German surface and submarine threats. This was done primarily by maintaining the "Otranto Barrage Line," which stretched across the Strait of Otranto between the southeast coast of Italy and west coast of Albania to close off the Adriatic Sea, where the Austro-Hungarian navy was based. According to Wise, "for the airmen the daily patrolling of the barrage was extremely monotonous. It was relieved by periodic bombing raids against U-boat bases in the Adriatic." On December 23, 1918, McLeod returned to England and then Canada.

New Brunswicker William Ernest Campbell also served in Italy. Born at St. George on December 11, 1895, Campbell was a twenty-one-year-old clerk with the Bank of Nova Scotia in Saint John by July 1914. He

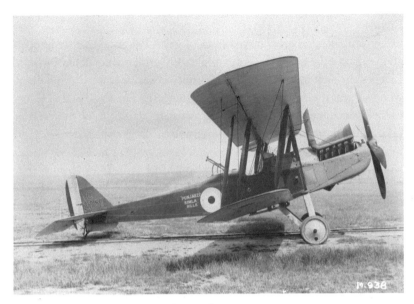

RE.8 aircraft. LAC-3390896

enlisted in the RFC Canada force on December 7, 1917, and after training in Ontario and Texas, he sailed to England and began his advanced training. At the end of October 1918, Campbell travelled to northern Italy, where he joined No. 34 Squadron and flew RE.8s on reconnaissance and bombing missions along the Isonzo front, where the British and French had several divisions deployed. He remained there after the Armistice until February 1919, when he rejoined the Home Establishment in Britain and then sailed for home in the summer.

Another New Brunswicker who served in the western Mediterranean and elsewhere was Robert McIntyre Coram, who was born in Saint John on April 12, 1886. By the time he enlisted in the RNAS in late 1915, he was a master mechanic and superintendent of a machine shop in Winnipeg. Throughout most of 1917, he was a chief petty officer working with seaplanes on various Royal Navy ships around Gibraltar and Malta. At the end of the year, he moved to Vendôme and was discharged in March 1918, whereupon he returned to Canada and became an instructor at Toronto.

Egypt

Other provincial airmen served in the Egypt–Palestine theatre of operations against the Ottoman Turks and their German allies. They included Lieutenant Jack Malcolm, a flying officer observer from Campbellton, who was sent to the Middle East in October 1917. He was based in Cairo, carrying out operations against enemy forces. In January 1918, he was fired upon while flying over Turkish positions. According to the *Daily Telegraph* in April 1918, "The shots went through his boots, but he escaped with a few scratches. His machine was disabled and he came to earth at the rate of thirty-five miles an hour. To prevent his machine from falling into the hands of the Turks he set fire to it and made for the woods." The report further related that it took him nine days to return to his headquarters, "hiding by day and travelling by night." He was about to be listed as missing when he arrived safely and reported in.

Lieutenant James Herbert Kirk also served in Egypt. The son of James T. Kirk, the collector of customs in Sussex, James was born on September 6, 1896. He became a bank teller and served with the 74th New Brunswick Rangers before the war. On October 14, 1915, he enlisted as a private in the 104th Battalion in Sussex and then on February 6, 1916, joined the 140th Battalion as a lieutenant. After sailing to England, he was posted to several units until proceeding on April 23, 1917, to the RFC at Reading to be trained as a flying officer observer on FE.2 and DH.4 aircraft. On May 30, 1917, he joined No. 25 Squadron in France and served with it until December 10, when he returned to England. A month later, he left for Egypt as an aviation instructor at the School of Aeronautics at Aboukir, near Alexandria, on the Mediterranean coast.

Macedonia

New Brunswickers also served in Macedonia in northern Greece against the Bulgarians and their German allies. Among them was Captain Edward John Cronin, who was born in Milltown, in Charlotte County, on April 14, 1890. He later lived in Saint John, where he worked as a merchant with Ward and Cronin, a gents' haberdashery store. In May 1911, he joined the provincial militia, becoming a lieutenant with the 62nd

Regiment, St. John Fusiliers. On December 6, 1915, he enlisted in the CEF's 104th Battalion as a lieutenant. Then, on February 15, 1916, he transferred to the 140th Battalion. In March, while serving in Fredericton, Cronin suffered a near-fatal injury. According to the *Daily Gleaner*, he was kicked by a horse while in the Provincial Exhibition Building and "suffered serious injuries about the head. The officer was on horseback and one of the soldiers was 'breaking in' another horse to such an extent that he bolted forward, throwing Lieut. Cronin into the snow. In dashing away the horse's hind heels struck the officer in the head and inflicted a nasty gash over the eye. Lieut. Cronin's escape from more serious injury was somewhat miraculous."

On September 25, 1916, he went overseas with the 140th, and after it disbanded he transferred to the 25th Nova Scotia Battalion and saw action in France. In early March 1917, he contracted appendicitis and trench fever and was sent to England, where he underwent an appendectomy. Upon recovering, he was seconded to the RFC at Reading and appointed temporary lieutenant on August 4, 1917. Between September and December, he was assigned to Nos. 49 and 20 Training Squadrons. Then, on January 8, 1918, he was sent to Egypt as an instructor at the aeronautical school. On February 12, he was made a lieutenant flying officer; on July 31, he was assigned to No. 94 Squadron; then, on September 17, he embarked for Macedonia. There, he joined No. 17 Squadron, a tactical reconnaissance unit, on the Struma River front in western Bulgaria, operating in support of Anglo-French forces driving north from Salonika. He flew against German aviators attached to the Bulgarian Army leading up to the armistice on that front that took effect on September 30. Cronin received the following recommendation from his commanding officer.

> This officer has been continually on active service since September 1918 flying on the Salonika front. He has carried out 80 special missions and bomb raids against the enemy with the greatest determination and devotion to duty. During the final attack from Salonika and Serbia Lieutenant Cronin with great skill and gallantry succeeded in observing large

enemy reinforcements assembling. He reported them at once [and] our army out manoeuvred [them] causing a general retirement…leading finally to the Bulgarian surrender. This officer was selected to convey despatches of greatest importance by aeroplane to the army commander operating in this area announcing the Bulgarian armistice. Lieutenant Cronin had a forced landing about 150 miles from his objective but conveyed his despatches by hand in a remarkable time with great determination and devotion to duty.

Another New Brunswicker who served in Macedonia was James Wilbur Macarthur. Born in Newcastle, Macarthur joined the RFC Canada scheme in Toronto on October 11, 1917, at age nineteen. After graduating in May 1918 as a second lieutenant, he went to England to undergo advanced training. On October 12, he joined No. 222 Squadron of the RAF's Aegean Group, and flew Sopwith Camels during the final days of Bulgaria's war. He remained in Salonika with No. 220 Squadron until April 1, 1919, when he sailed to England. His return to Canada was delayed when he was admitted to hospital in late May, where he remained for the next several months.

Russia

After the Bolsheviks overthrew the Kerensky government in November 1917 (October in the Julian calendar) and then signed the Treaty of Brest–Litovsk in March 1918, ending Russia's war with Germany, more than a dozen Allied countries, including Britain and France, sent troops to continue the war against Germany and Turkey in the region. At the same time, some nations decided to support the nascent opposition forming against the Reds throughout the former Russian Empire by anti-Bolshevik (White) forces and ethnic minorities that had declared their independence. By early 1918, a civil war had developed throughout the region that would continue until 1923.

At least four New Brunswickers served in Russia. Three of them, George Willis Jones of Moncton, James Vans McDonald from Campbellton, and

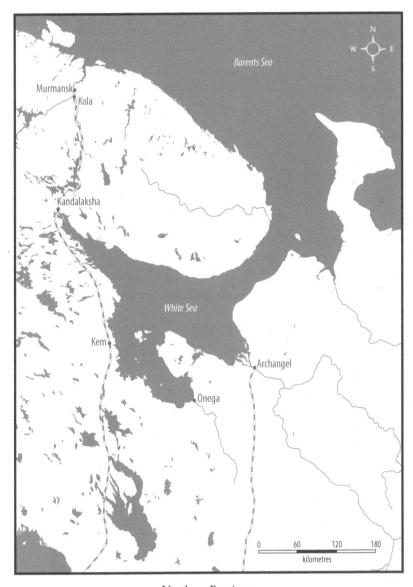

Northern Russia. MB

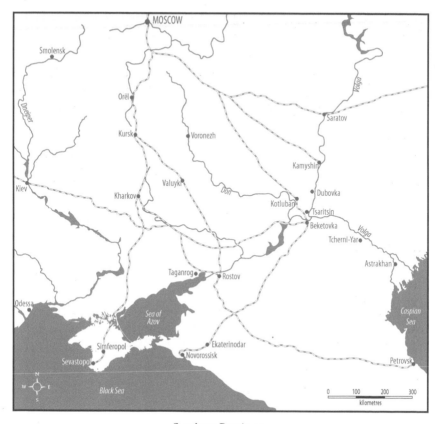

Southern Russia. MB

Frank O. Soden were part of the Allied force code-named "Elope" that went to Archangel in north Russia beginning in July 1918 to continue the fight against the Germans and support the forces that opposed the Reds.

George Jones was born in Summerside, Prince Edward Island, on May 13, 1891, but by 1901 he was living with his family in Sunny Brae (now part of Moncton). By the time he enlisted in Saint John as a private in the 115th Battalion in February 1916, James was working as a merchant for his father, Clarence L. Jones, a prominent businessman and developer in Moncton. Clarence was known for introducing the pasteurization of milk

3 Cross Street, in the Moncton neighbourhood of Sunny Brae, where George Jones grew up. Moncton Museum Collection

around the area through his milk factory and general store. At the time of his enlistment, George was married to Bessie Millar, and a few months later their daughter was born. In July 1916, he sailed with the 115th to England, where he transferred to several different units throughout late 1916 and early 1917. By May 1917, he had been promoted to company sergeant major as a bombing instructor. Then, on October 1, he was transferred to No. 2 Cadet Wing of the RFC at Hastings. In July 1918, Jones was gazetted as a temporary second lieutenant. On September 8, he joined the "Elope" Squadron as an RE.8 pilot, and a few weeks later sailed for northern Russia as part of a squadron draft. On October 2, Jones joined the expeditionary force where he served until mid-May 1919, whereupon he was slowly repatriated back to England, arriving in Liverpool at the end of June.

Another provincial airman who served in north Russia was James Vans McDonald, who was born in Campbellton on October 31, 1892. He served in the New Brunswick militia's 73rd Regiment for three years, attending camp at Sussex, where he took a St. John's Ambulance course prior to moving to Vernon, British Columbia, and becoming a druggist. McDonald was a student at McGill University when he enlisted in the Canadian Army Medical Corps' No. 4 Field Ambulance as a private on November 15, 1914, at Esquimalt. He sailed to England on the SS *Northland* on April 18. In July, he went to France with his unit and became a sergeant shortly afterwards. After being admitted to hospital suffering from a hernia and undergoing surgery, McDonald returned to England to convalesce. In August 1917, he began cadet training with the RFC, flying various aircraft, including the SPAD, Sopwith Pup, and Dolphin, while at Gosport. Upon graduating and appointment as a flying officer, in January 1918 he briefly became an assistant instructor. Throughout much of 1918, he served with various squadrons, including No. 1 Canadian at the time of the Armistice. After several other postings, McDonald sailed on July 3, 1919, for northern Russia to join the expeditionary force's squadron.

In 1918, Britain also began supplying White forces in southern Russia with munitions, training, and direct military support, including operational squadrons from the RAF. The first of these airmen began working in November with White forces commanded by General Anton Deniken, a former czarist officer, in their struggle against the Red Army. The focus of much of this activity was the zone between the Black and Caspian Seas. In April 1919, half of No. 47 Squadron was sent from Salonika to the area, later reinforced by ten officers from No. 17 Squadron, among them Edward Cronin, the final New Brunswicker to serve in Russia.

In March 1919, Cronin was sent from Macedonia to Constantinople, then under Allied military occupation, flying the 370 miles in three hours. On April 20, he joined No. 47 Squadron and by July 13 was on his way to the Caucasus region. In mid-June, the Canadian wartime ace, Major Raymond Collishaw, had taken command of the 47th, and by July they had begun assembling three flights of older DH.9 two-seater bombers. Cronin flew missions with the squadron's "C" Flight, operating from an airfield at Beketovka near Tsaritsyn (later Stalingrad, now Volgograd), a large port on the Volga River, in support of the White forces' Caucasian Army commanded by General Pyotr Wrangel.

Between July and November, Cronin carried out various roles. On July 17, he flew an important reconnaissance mission to Kamyshin, on

162. 'C' Flight, No. 47 Squadron, RAF at Beketovka, summer 1919. Identified are front row from left: Lieutenant Mercer; Lieutenant Simmons; unknown former RNAS pilot; unknown. Middle row from left: two unknown White Russian officers; Captain Frogley ('C' Flight commander); Major Collishaw (Commanding 47 Squadron); Captain Anderson; unknown; Lieutenant Elliot. Back row from left: unknown; Lieutenant Hatchett; unknown; Lieutenant Mitchell. (Public domain)

No. 47 Squadron's "C" Flight officers at Beketovka, Russia;
Lieutenant Edward Cronin is likely sitting in the middle row,
second from the right. LAC PA-203556

the Volga River 110 miles north of Tsaritsyn. On July 25, he and the flight commander, Captain Sidney G. Frogley, bombed Red troops near Tcherni-Yar, ninety miles southeast of Tsaritsyn, and attacked a fleet of barges the Reds used to move troops and supplies up and down the Volga, the main transportation artery in the area. During a bombing raid on August 20, Cronin was attacked by a Red Air Force pilot. According to Cronin's combat report, quoted in John T. Smith's *Gone to Russia to Fight: The RAF in South Russia 1918–1920*:

0810 hours over Tcherni-Yar an enemy Nieuport was seen to dive on me on my right rear. My front gun was not working. I circled round to give my observer (Lieut. A. Mercer) a field of fire. After 10 minutes fighting during which 4 bursts of fire was [*sic*] exchanged from about 50 to 100 yards, the enemy was seen to go down in control after a burst of fire into his left wing, out of which splinters flew. He was observed to go down over the marshes N.E. of Tcherni-Yar and was then lost sight of. He was undoubtedly badly shot up.

On August 28, Cronin attacked an armoured car, killing the driver and overturning the vehicle in the ditch.

By September, the Reds had pushed closer to Tsaritsyn from the north, capturing the town of Dubovka. On the seventh, Cronin and Mercer made a two-and-a-half-hour flight north on a bombing raid. Mercer noted in his logbook: "Two enemy machines seen. They ran away." On September 16, they and another plane carried out a raid on Dubovka during which a Red Air Force Nieuport attacked them. According to Cronin's combat report:

While over Chirokoe we were flying north when an enemy machine was observed four miles in rear and flying towards us. The two DHs immediately turned to meet him. The enemy scout dived in between the tails of our machines and was met with heavy and effective cross fire from Lewis Guns, his propeller was seen to stop and he went down in a long steep dive followed by our machines, which were unable to overtake him. Enemy scout was last seen ten feet above ground over Dubovka flying south.

In subsequent flights in October, Cronin and other planes from "C" Flight bombed a Red artillery battery, scoring a direct hit with a 112-lb. bomb. On October 13, he attacked an armoured train. At the end of the month, with war weariness spreading among the RAF personnel and opposition to the intervention growing in Britain, the flight was disbanded and the airmen moved to the rear for evacuation.

In November 1919, Cronin departed for home, finally arriving back in New Brunswick on January 2, 1920, after a long journey via Constantinople, Salonika, Rome, Marseilles, Paris, London, and finally New York. The *Saint John Globe* speculated that by then he had "perhaps seen as much service on many of England's far flung battle fronts as any New Brunswick soldier." On April 1, 1920, Cronin was awarded the DFC for his conduct during both the Great War and the Allied intervention in the Russian Civil War. According to his DFC citation, he "had taken part in eighty raids on enemy territory, displaying great ability and gallantry. On July 17, 1919, at Kamyshin (Volga) he carried out an important reconnaissance with great skill and daring flying as low as 500 feet at a critical time. Lt. Cronin previously rendered gallant service during the Bulgarian retreat in the autumn of 1918." He also received the Russian Cross of St. George.

Chapter Five

Casualties

Air operations were dangerous and required much skill and courage. Nevertheless, many New Brunswick airmen became casualties. Some were wounded or injured in action, but a significant number died in flying accidents or combat.

Wounded Airmen

Throughout the war, 1,130 Canadian airmen were injured or wounded in action. They included at least eleven New Brunswickers. Among the earliest wounded flyers was Lieutenant Robert Shives from Campbellton. On December 29, 1915, he was promoted to flying officer and then, on February 1, 1916, he joined No. 5 Squadron, a reconnaissance unit in France, as a pilot. On April 29, he was wounded in action. A report in the *Moncton Daily Times* in early August recounted some of the details: "Lieut. Shives was wounded ... in a fight with a German airman over enemy lines. He was selected to make a flight to ascertain the position of the enemy, and while returning to the British lines was attacked by a German aviator. In the fight that followed he was wounded in the right leg and side and, although he had reached a point twelve miles over the German lines, he was able to guide his machine back to base safely." After a few days in hospital in France, Shives was invalided to England, where

Lieutenant Robert Shives seated in the cockpit of his aircraft.
Courtesy of Patti Craig

Wounded in Action
Creaghan, Thomas Cyril, November 20, 1917
Eveleigh, Edgar Percy, September 15, 1918
Hanning, James Edward, March 28, 1918
Kitchen, George Walter, October 15, 1918
Landry, Wilfred Andrew, February 15, 1917
Richardson, Leonard, July 19, 1918
Ritchie, Louis McCoskery, February 24, 1918
Russell, J. Douglas, September 8, 1918
Shives, Robert Kilgour, April 29, 1916
Taylor, Gordon Winslow, March 13, 1918
Travis, Frederick Pauley Joseph, August 2, 1918
Wootten, George Bates, October 30, 1918

he spent many weeks recovering. In recognition of his gallant conduct returning the twenty-five miles to his aerodrome after being wounded, his squadron commander recommended him for the DCM. Although he did not receive the award, he was promoted to captain on June 1, 1916.

Another wounded airman was Flight Lieutenant G. Walter Kitchen from Fredericton. Kitchen enlisted in the RFC Canada scheme in November 1917 and soon reported for duty at Toronto. He spent three or four months in Texas taking a flying course and after returning to Canada went to Beamsville, Ontario, where he completed his training as a pilot. Out of a class of 195 cadets, he was the first to get his wings and commission. In May 1918, he was sent to England and after completing his advanced training he was assigned to patrolling the coastline. According to the *Daily Gleaner*, "on account of performing his duties so admirably he was sent to France," where he became involved in combat operations. During one mission, the manifold on his plane was shot off and he made a forced descent, "taking the tops off the trees and making a perfect landing behind his own lines." After the manifold was replaced, he went back up, "delivering fully on the people whom he supposed shot his manifold off." On another mission, five pieces of shrapnel passed through his wings.

On October 15, Walter was wounded while flying near Ypres. After being sent to London, he wrote a lengthy letter to his parents on October 22 describing the action in which he was incapacitated.

> My Dear Mother and Father—I am convalescing at the R.A.F. Hospital 37, Bryanston Sq., which is very comfortable. I got hit last Monday morning, but did not get back to Blighty till late Friday night. I wired you Sunday morning, which, no doubt, you have received. I was doing long distance patrol, with my flight commander, back of Courtrai, when we were attacked by seven Fokkers. My observer got hit at the first of the fight. We then started a running fight back to our lines. Just at crossing our lines my flight commander was shot down in flames. About the same time I got a bullet just touching my right wrist, which is only a scratch but broke the tip of the steroid [*sic*] which put me

out of commission. I was then followed down to about 300 feet, when they shot my controls away, and I crashed, just north of Ledegem on the Roulers-Menin road, pretty badly shaken up in the crash, but feel O.K. now.

I had a small splinter of bullet just in front of the shin of my leg, but it has been removed. I was very lucky getting within our lines, as our troops only advanced over this ground about an hour before I crashed. As it was the first day of the second Ypres show [the Battle of Courtrai, which began on October 14, 1918], my hand and leg were dressed and I went back to my quarters. My observer died in the casualty clearing station, which made me feel awfully bad.

I am able to get about at present and am trying to take in all the shows in town.

Walter

P.S. — Do not expect many letters till my hand is in better condition.

P.P.S. — Tell Dr. Irvine that I lost a couple of his teeth.

On July 19, 1918, Lieutenant Leonard Richardson was wounded during a mission when No. 74 Squadron was acting as an escort to Bristol fighters from No. 20 Squadron that were dropping bombs on Roulers, in Belgium.

The Bristols dropped their bombs and immediately after we got into a real sized dog-fight. I was on the west side of the formation, the side nearest our lines, even though 12 miles away. This gave me a false sense of security because rarely did the Hun cross our formation, they preferred to fight from their side.

We were revving all over the dog-fight when I saw a Hun on the tail of one of our machines. I dove on the Hun until he went down. I was so intent on watching, trying to get a true confirmation, that I forgot my tail, so when I zoomed up to maintain altitude, I was very much surprised to receive a cockpit full of bullets.

Some stout Hun who had crossed the formation, met me at the top of my zoom. His first burst got me through the shoulder, shot my main petrol, one of my magnetos and instruments. I remembered [my flight leader's] advice in such a situation — joy stick full forward, engine full on, dive like hell and get away.

I turned in my seat to watch the Hun who followed me for a bit; he duplicated my maneuvers but I was able to prevent him setting another straight shot at me. I had turned on my auxiliary tank which I knew should provide enough petrol to get across the lines.

Shortly after crossing into friendly territory, he crash-landed. "My machine turned over and broke up but my only injury in the landing was, I skinned my knuckles! My machine was not worth salvaging!" Richardson had come down near the camp of an American machine-gun battalion, some of whom helped him out of the wreckage and got him to their medical tent. There, the medical officer bandaged his wound, "gave me a large drink," and called a field ambulance, which took him to No. 44 Casualty Clearing Station near Berque, on the Channel coast, where he had his wound dressed. "The war was over for a while."

The next day, Richardson travelled by ambulance train to Boulogne. "What a hellish ride. The train was full of seriously wounded soldiers groaning and crying and yelling as we bumped along." He was taken by stretcher and ambulance to No. 8 British Red Cross Hospital, where he shared a room with two other officers. "It seemed like Heaven to me. It is unbelievable to have a good-looking Nurse make a fuss over me, whom I suppose is the umpteenth man she has cared for. She even told me she heard of my 'pukka' fight, which of course is a lot of 'Bull' but I loved it."

A few days later Richardson celebrated his twenty-fourth birthday. Reflecting on all that had happened, he wrote: "I have escaped death and have a new lease of life. But why me? I wonder why one is taken and another left." On July 23, he had another operation where the wound was swabbed out and sown up "like a barbed wire entanglement. It's about as effective too: hurts like Hell." The pain kept him awake some nights. To pass the time, he read magazines, attended band concerts, got his haircut in bed, talked with the other patients, watched nearby seaplanes, and tried "to kid the nurses."

On August 1, he departed for England on a hospital ship, disembarked at Dover, and then proceeded by train to London, where the returning wounded were met with an elaborate reception: "young girls with flowers, Old Girls with coffee—it made me feel that I was the only soldier in the world who had ever been wounded.... It's English—it's wonderful—it's worth it."

Even though wounded, some of these airmen carried on with their missions and were later recommended for decorations. They included John Edward Hanning, who was born on November 30, 1889, in Fredericton, graduated from the Provincial Normal School, and taught school at St. Stephen until moving west. He served with the militia's Corps of Guides for a year. On August 2, 1916, he enlisted in the Canadian Engineers at Ottawa as a lieutenant. After arriving in Britain, Hanning joined the RFC's No. 1 School of Aeronautics at Reading on July 16, 1917, and underwent training as an observer. On September 9, he proceeded to France as a flying officer (observer), where he served with No. 59 Squadron until April 11, 1918.

Hanning was awarded the Military Cross "for extreme gallantry and resourcefulness" during a mission he flew in which he was wounded. The recommendation stated:

> On 28th March 1918, while on patrol with 2nd Lieutenant Christian as pilot, [Hanning] endeavoured to shoot down a hostile balloon over Miraumont [in the Somme area]. His machine was at once attacked by a hostile scout, and after firing 90 rounds his gun jammed. Although wounded in the leg by an explosive bullet, he rectified the trouble, and was about to fit a new drum on the gun when a bullet hit it and destroyed it. The enemy aircraft then dived underneath the tail, did a climbing turn, and again attacked. Lieutenant Hanning again repaired his gun and fired a long burst into the enemy scout. The enemy pilot

collapsed in his seat and his machine spun to the ground. The controls of Lieutenant Hanning's machine were, by this time, so damaged that his pilot could not fly it. He, however, fitted the dual control and succeeded in bringing the machine back to our lines and landing it. By his courage and determination, though wounded, Lieutenant Hanning undoubtedly saved the life of his pilot.

And in the process, he shot down his attacker. According to the *Daily Telegraph*, Hanning received his MC from King George V personally at Aldershot on June 8.

Psychological Wounds

Some airmen suffered both physical and psychological wounds. Captain George Alvah Good incurred lasting physical and psychological effects from a near fatal crash during his service. Born in Woodstock on May 26, 1896, the son of Major Frank A. Good, a well-known militia officer in the area, he grew up in Fredericton. When war came, Alvah was a second-year student at UNB with previous militia experience with both the 67th and 71st Regiments. On September 8, 1914, he joined the company the 71st contributed to form the Composite Battalion being raised throughout the Maritimes to defend Halifax. After several months of home service, Good went to England in June 1915 in command of an overseas draft from the unit. He joined the 23rd Battalion,

Lieutenant Alvah Good.
MC 300/MS 69/23, PANB

becoming the battalion signalling officer in August. On January 17, 1916, he was assigned to the 28th Battalion in Belgium as their signalling officer. Near the end of February, he attended a week-long training course and then rejoined his unit at the front. In April, Good was part of 2nd Canadian Division's first major action during the Battle of the St. Eloi Craters. A letter he wrote to his parents about his experiences during the battle, published in the *Saint John Globe*, described how the psychological shock of intense combat affected him and how his religious faith sustained him.

I have just been through the busiest two weeks I ever dreamed of. For two days we were working under horrible conditions in a bad trench under fire with practically nothing to eat or drink, and no sleep for two days and three nights. Also the last evening Fritz gave us what an artillery expert has said was the heaviest bombardment ever put over on this front. We lost a lot of men and worked horribly hard, but there are a lot of fortunate ones who have got out and among them myself. And to speak along a line I seldom refer to — if I hadn't been a very firm believer of an Almighty and wise hand governing the whole of our small affairs and the ever-present Comforter I'm sure I would have gone crazy over the strain I was through and the sights I saw. I think you can understand what I mean all right. But I don't want to cause you any anxiety — and it's all over now, cheer up.

Then, on October 3, he was wounded by a shell fragment that cut his thigh, and he was hospitalized for a short time.

On November 8, 1916, Good was seconded to the RFC, underwent training on BE.2E and BE.2A aircraft, and was confirmed as a flying officer (observer) on February 15, 1917. In May, he joined the Home Establishment as an assistant instructor and later was sent to France, where he flew missions as an observer until June 1918, when he returned to England to undergo pilot training. During his training, he crashed at least once while making a practice landing. Then, on October 23,

(above) "My First Crash!" Lieutenant Alvah Good's aircraft after a practice landing during training. MC 300/MS 69/23, PANB

(right) Lieutenant Alvah Good at Throwley, Kent. MC 300/MS 69/23, PANB

1918, Good was involved in a near-fatal airplane accident at Throwley, Kent, which had lasting effects on him. According to a later medical report, "his present trouble commenced with [this] 'crash.' Previous to this he had exceptional nerve and was considered to be a daring flier." During the accident, the left temporal area of his head was struck and he sustained a fractured skull. He was hospitalized at the Fort Pitt Military Hospital in Chatham, Kent, where he remained unconscious for six weeks. He slowly convalesced through November and December. On March 25, 1919, he was again admitted to hospital, where he was diagnosed with neurasthenia, also known as shell shock at the time. He was released shortly afterwards, now unfit for further service, and on March 31 sailed home to Canada.

Another airman adversely affected by his combat experiences was Flight Lieutenant Louis Ritchie of Saint John. Born on September 12, 1894, at the time of his enlistment Ritchie was a twenty-one-year-old law student who had served for three years with the militia's 62nd Regiment. On August 15, 1916, he enlisted as a private with the 236th Battalion (The New Brunswick Kilties) and received a lieutenant's commission a month later. On September 18, he sailed aboard the SS *Olympic* to England, where he spent time with several reserve units until being sent to France on April 27, 1917, initially to the 87th Battalion and then the 26th New Brunswick Battalion. On October 12, he was seconded to the RFC as a second lieutenant, and a month later became an observer on probation. He underwent training at Reading and Winchester, and on January 1, 1918, became a corps observer. On January 4, Ritchie joined No. 5 Squadron in France.

On February 24, Ritchie was seriously wounded near Arras. A report in the *Daily Telegraph* recorded: "The machine was flying over the German lines and was hit. The machine became ablaze and they were forced to descend. However, before the plane landed the pilot and Lieutenant Ritchie suffered severe burns, the latter also being shot in the foot. Lieutenant Ritchie recovered but the pilot succumbed to his injuries." According to other reports, the plane fell nearly 3,000 feet on fire before landing. He was evacuated to No. 57 Casualty Clearing Station and then hospitals in Le Touquet, France, London, and Moffat, Scotland, to recover from the gunshot wound to his left ankle, burns to his face and hands, and shock. According to his medical files, he complained of moderate headaches, lassitude, weakened resistance to fatigue, and difficulty concentrating his attention. A specialist's report stated: "Noises startle him more easily than formerly. He finds himself restless, picking at clothing and things with his fingers, fidgety. Sleep is fairly good and weight about normal, though he has lost some twenty pounds gained in training. The symptoms seem to be abating and I believe will continue to do so. They are, doubtless, neurasthenic, following in the wake of shock undergone and for which he was in hospital." In August, 1918, Ritchie returned to Canada and was discharged.

Lieutenant John Warren Price from Moncton also suffered from the psychological stress of air operations. As we saw in chapter 3, in the summer of 1917 Price joined No. 100 Squadron as an observer, carrying out bombing raids deep into Germany. In late September, he was briefly admitted to No. 39 Stationary Hospital suffering from a concussion, but soon returned to duty. Then, as the *Moncton Daily Times* reported, on November 12, he wrote to his parents from France about being hospitalized suffering from the effects of prolonged night operations against the Germans.

> Am once more in hospital at the base. You see I had been moved away South and we were doing what the London people had been crying so long [for] — reprisals. However, I have [been] well into Germany, and you see it is past my time for going to Blighty to take a pilot's course, but they did not send me soon enough — so now they must give me a few weeks in hospital. Have been here since the 5th, but leave tomorrow for England and get hospital there for a while. My nerves are in pretty bad shape, as I have been over the top 38 times and have 35 [bombing missions] to my credit, and at night that is going some.
>
> My best friends have gone west [killed in action], and one of the very best was brought down in Hunland two weeks ago. Poor chap! He was coming with me next week, but that's the game.

On November 17, Price wrote again, this time from the Princess Christian Hospital in London, where he had been admitted suffering from debility. "This rest, I think, was coming to me, as I have dropped bombs on the Huns 35 times and three times well into Germany, and if you hear of any one observer who had been there that many times at night, just let him have my place at home. It was fair H--- at the last, not that it was any worse than at the first. But one can only stand so much and then one goes 'wankey.'"

In February 1918, Price was sent home on sick leave, arriving in Moncton unexpectedly on the fifteenth. The *Moncton Daily Times* wrote a sympathetic account of his recent illness for its readers.

> Lieut. Price escaped through his many hazardous flights without any injury but as will be readily understood the nature of his work in the air does not tend to make the nerves any stronger and, after making a great many dangerous trips over the lines of the Hun and being exposed to the full force of all their efforts to bring him down Lieut. Price at last found that he was badly in need of a little rest and relief from his dangerous duties. He was sent over to England where he entered a hospital to recuperate. From there he was granted a furlough home where he arrived yesterday afternoon.

Following the end of his leave, Price was posted to the RAF Armament School in Hamilton, Ontario, where he trained observers. In late September, he was admitted to the Hamilton Military Hospital suffering from pneumonia and died on October 9.

Price's elder brother, Harold, also served in the RFC and suffered similar adverse effects. Born on September 3, 1884, in Moncton, Harold Newton Price became an electrical engineer, and was general superintendent and chief engineer with the Moncton Tramway Electricity and Gas Company. In November 1915, he joined the militia's 8th Princess Louise's New Brunswick Hussars, and then on May 5, 1916, became a lieutenant and platoon commander in the CEF's 185th Battalion (Cape Breton Highlanders). They sailed for England in October 1916, and on August 14, 1917, he was seconded to the RFC at Reading and underwent training until March 13, 1918, when he was appointed a flying officer. On June 26, he joined No. 80 Squadron, where he flew Sopwith Camels, mostly in a ground-attack role. According to his air service file, on July 26, "at Chateau-Thierry, France his machine (Camel Scout) crashed to the ground in flames. He was unconscious for some time," and suffered a serious wound to the back of his head. On July 31, he was admitted to No.

14 General Hospital in Wimereux, France, suffering from a concussion. On August 17, he was discharged and granted three weeks' sick leave but was readmitted on September 11. A hospital case history report stated: "during October 1918 he began to get up and walk about hospital. At that time patient was very nervous, would jump on the least noise, could not sleep, had war dreams (falling from plane), whole body was shaken. While in hospital there was some improvement." Afterwards, he was sent to hospitals in England for more than two months, and then in mid-December he returned to Canada.

Price continued to receive medical care at home. On February 5, 1919, still suffering from "nervous debility," he underwent assessment in Saint John. He was found to be physically "well-nourished but nervous." He had constant pain at the back of his head and neck, and intense headaches that compelled him to go to bed. He also suffered from insomnia, getting only two to four hours' sleep at night on average. He "feels nervous and is easily excited," and was unable to resume his occupation. In the opinion of a specialist, the pain at the back of his neck was "the result of the nervous condition which condition requires rest...the nervous condition is the result of active service."

On April 1, Price was admitted to the military hospital at Ste-Anne-de-Bellevue, outside Montreal, where he was treated for neurasthenia. He revealed that, since returning home, he "has been worried very much by the recent death of his father and brother [both had died during the influenza pandemic, leaving his mother widowed]. Feels that he is unable to resume former occupation on account of inability to work more than a few hours a day. Also stated that since he has been out of hospital his condition has progressed very rapidly." Price was discharged from military service in July 1919 and by 1921 had returned to work.

Accidental Deaths

Numerous deaths occurred among these airmen under various circumstances. Some were caused by accidents. Following his wounding in France, hospitalization in England, and furlough back home, on September 26, 1916, Captain Robert Shives joined No. 51 Squadron, a home defence unit

Lieutenant John (Jack) Clarence Hanson
(Daily Gleaner)

based at Thetford, Norfolk, organized to protect Britain from German Zeppelin raids. There, he became a flight commander. Three days later, he was killed in an accident while examining a Lewis gun. According to an inquest, "the evidence showed there were three spent cartridges [in the gun], and [an] explosion shattered his head."

Others died during flying accidents, the causes of which were often unknown but were likely due to mechanical failures in the aircraft or pilot error. The killed included John Thomas Gibson, who was born and grew up in Marysville, attended Fredericton High School, and enlisted in the 71st York Regiment in 1906 as a private. He attended UNB, graduating in 1910 with a degree in civil engineering, and worked for the Dominion public works department in Saint John and Fredericton. He was commissioned as a lieutenant in the 71st in July 1916, and in September was appointed a recruiting officer for Queens and Sunbury counties. In May 1917, he joined the RFC Canada scheme in Toronto, and after receiving his wings went overseas in September to complete his training. On February 10, 1918, the twenty-nine-year-old Gibson died in hospital from injuries received in a fall during a practice flight. He was buried in the Yatesbury (All Saints) Churchyard Cemetery in Wiltshire, England.

Several incidents occurred during test flights at the front. Among the losses was John (Jack) Clarence Hanson, born on May 27, 1893, in Sussex, the only child of Rupert and Gussie Hanson. Rupert was an inspector of schools, and the family moved around the province before finally settling in Fredericton. As a result, Jack was educated at Bathurst and Chatham Grammar Schools before attending UNB in Fredericton and graduating with a Bachelor of Arts in 1913. As a report in the *Kings County Record* shows, he was an outstanding student: at Bathurst he won the high school entrance exam medal, at Chatham the graduation medal, and at UNB he was awarded the Alumni Medal for best Latin essay and the Governor General's medal for efficiency in science.

Afterwards, Hanson became a teacher at a school in Grand Falls and then principal of the Consolidated School at Riverside in Albert County. He also served in the pre-war militia as a staff sergeant in the 71st Regiment and lieutenant in the 74th, attending summer camp at Sussex for three years. On March 12, 1916, he joined the 104th Battalion as a lieutenant and sailed for England on June 28. On January 26, 1917, he was struck off strength with the 104th and transferred to the 13th New Brunswick Reserve Battalion for posting to the front. On April 23, Hanson was seconded to the RFC, underwent training as an observer at Reading, and on June 10 joined No. 55 Squadron in France. On July 14, Hanson was mortally injured in a flying accident and died later that day at No. 10 Stationary Hospital at Saint-Omer. He was buried at Longuenesse (Saint-Omer) Souvenir Cemetery.

The Hansons learned about the circumstances of Jack's death from a letter dated July 17, 1917, written by Major J.S. Baldwin, Officer Commanding No. 55 Squadron.

Dear Mr. Hanson

I regret to have to write to you and inform you that your son, J.C. Hanson, was killed on the 14th inst., in an aeroplane accident. He was up with his pilot on a test flight near the aerodrome when for some reason the machine's nose dived into the ground and both occupants were killed. It is impossible to say why the accident occurred, as the machine was in perfect order and there is nothing to show why it should have suddenly fallen. I am exceedingly sorry it should have happened so as it seems such a waste of a useful officer. Your son was doing exceedingly well in this squadron and was a good observer. Please accept my deepest sympathy with you and the rest of his family.

Other fatalities occurred because of flying accidents during active operations. Among them was Flight Lieutenant Jarvis Oldfield McLellan from Saint John. Before enlisting in November 1917 at age nineteen, McLellan went to school in the city and became a clerk at the Bank of Nova Scotia in Haymarket Square. He completed his lieutenant's courses in Halifax in musketry and machine-gun operations and was attached to the 28th Dragoons before joining the air service in Toronto. He spent the winter of 1917/18 training in Texas, and after graduating became an instructor. According to the *Daily Telegraph*, however, "this was somewhat against the ambitious lad's desire's as he was eager for real warlike service." In May 1918, McLellan went overseas, where he joined the RAF's No. 256 Squadron on June 18 at Elford, in northern England. There, he undertook coastal scout duty in DH.6s, searching for German submarines near Newcastle. On July 8, he was seriously injured in a flying accident, and died two days later at the No. 1 Northern General Hospital in Newcastle.

McLellan's family first learned of his accident when a cable was sent to his father, J. Verner McLellan of the city's Registrar Office, on July 9 notifying him that his only child was in hospital, but reporting that he was "in no immediate danger." A short time later, however, another cable arrived with news of Jarvis's death. According to the *Daily Telegraph*, Mr.

McLellan "was completely crushed." He had refrained from notifying his wife, Florence, who was spending the summer in Sussex, of the first cable, assuming it "might be converted into a still more hopeful message.... Sadly enough the reverse has been the case." Friends notified Mrs. McLellan of these turn of events and accompanied her home.

Killed or Missing in Action

Operational flying also led to many fatal casualties among New Brunswick airmen. According to Wise's *Canadian Airmen*, Canadian airmen incurred 1,388 fatal casualties. Most were lost in action. At least thirteen New Brunswickers were killed in action or listed as missing in action, while another three died from their wounds.

Among the earliest fatalities was Second Lieutenant Morden Mowat from Campbellton, who was killed in action on May 16, 1916. After arriving in England in early December 1915, Mowat reported to No. 3 Reserve Squadron at Shoreham, and then moved on to No. 23 Squadron at Gosport shortly before they crossed to France on March 16, 1916. Then, on April 24, he transferred to "B" Flight of No. 11 Squadron, stationed near Arras. There, Mowat flew Bristol Scouts alongside Lieutenant Albert Ball, the future ace and Victoria Cross recipient, who joined the unit a few weeks later. On the morning of May 16, Mowat crashed his plane. According to the diary of Flight Sergeant W.E.G. Crisfold, "B" Flight's chief mechanic, "Lt. Mowat lost his engine — while spiraling down and planed into the roof of A Flight hangar. Lt. Mowat was not even shaken up. The Machine hit between the last two stays at the end and was held by canvas and the planes. [He got] down alright [but] all the planes were done in." During another flight later that day with two other planes from his squadron, Mowat, in Bristol Scout 5301, came under fire from a German anti-aircraft battery and then was attacked by German ace Oberleutnant Max Immelmann. Mowat's plane fell into a spin and crashed into the ground behind the German lines at the village of Izel-lès-Équerchin, east of Vimy Ridge. Mowat's body and the remains of his machine were brought to a nearby German base. Mowat was initially buried in a cemetery in Arleux-en-Gohelle, close to where he crashed and died, but after the war, the body

Killed or Missing in Action
Babbitt, Thomas Emerson, July 15, 1918
Barr, Herbert Carrick, December 11, 1916
Dawson, Stephen Arthur, August 10, 1918
Gilmour, Arthur Clair, March 6, 1918
Graves, Charles Lee, April 24, 1917
Harmon, Burdette, May 10, 1918
Johnston, Robin Louis, May 9, 1918
Kent, William Morley, February 21, 1918
McNally, Percy Byron, August 13, 1917
Melanson, Albert Joseph, May 9, 1918
Mowat, Morden, May 16, 1916
Parlee, George William Hugh, August 20, 1918
Rankin, Franklin Sharp, October 23, 1916

Died of Wounds
Higgs, Lloyd Alfred, October 7, 1918
Jack, R. Lawrence M., February 26, 1917
Parks, Herbert Clifford, December 19, 1918

Grave of Second Lieutenant Morden Mowat,
Cabaret-Rouge British Cemetery,
Souchez, France. Author's photo

was exhumed and reburied at the Cabaret-Rouge British Cemetery, near Souchez.

Two other airmen killed early on were Lieutenants Burdette Harmon and Franklin Rankin, both from Woodstock. After being seconded to the RFC from his service with the 52nd Battalion in May 1917, Harmon was sent back to England, where he attended ground school for pilot trainees at the School of Aeronautics at Reading and then the Central Flying School at Upavon, in Wiltshire. He was awarded his wings in September, and at the beginning of October joined No. 56 Squadron, made famous by legendary aces Albert Ball and James McCudden. There, he flew single-seat SE.5 scouts. On November 23, Harmon was credited with shooting down a German two-seater south of the Arras-Cambrai Road. Then, on December 3, he was wounded for the third time — in the face on this occasion — hospitalized, then given a three-month furlough, during which he returned home. On May 3, 1918, he rejoined the 56th, and on May 10 went missing during aerial combat east of Corbie, near Amiens. His death was later confirmed by German sources. The circumstances of Harmon's loss were recorded in a letter sent to his widow by the squadron's commanding officer and published in the *Carleton Sentinel*.

> I am very sorry indeed to have to tell you that I can give you no hope for your husband who was reported "missing" on the 10th of May, 1918. When on an offensive patrol five miles behind the German lines at 7:50 in the evening on the 10th, he attacked 10 enemy scouts [fighter planes], one of which he brought down in flames. While engaged in this he was attacked by others from behind, one of which hit him in its first few shots, and finally his machine broke up.

Burdette Harmon is buried at the Villers-Bretonneux Military Cemetery, near Amiens.

Lieutenant Franklin Rankin, who died on October 23, 1916, was born in Woodstock on July 31, 1894, and educated in local schools, the Rothesay Boys' School, and the Royal Military College in Kingston between 1911 and 1914. Before the war, he was an officer in the provincial militia's 28th New Brunswick Dragoons. At the outset of the war, he joined the First Contingent's 1st Field Company, CE, left for Valcartier in late August, and sailed overseas in October. Beginning in June 1915, he served with the company at the front until being seconded to the RFC in May 1916. On July 21, 1916, he qualified as an observer, and ten days later transferred to No. 18 Squadron in France. Since April, the squadron had been

Lieutenant Franklin Rankin. NBM X12555

flying army cooperation missions in a new, two-seater "pusher" FE.2B aircraft. In this type, both the pilot and observer sat forward of the propellor and wings, with the observer in the nose handling two Lewis machine guns capable of firing in wide, unobstructed arcs. During the Somme offensive, the squadron was attached to the British Cavalry Corps. According to historian Andrew Godefroy, Rankin received most of his observer/gunner training with No. 18 Squadron, including learning Morse code communication, how to operate a wireless set and camera, and fire his Lewis guns.

Rankin flew missions with his pilot, Second Lieutenant F.L. Barnard, throughout the Somme offensive. In *Canadian Airmen*, Wise describes a patrol on October 20 when, while flying their FE.2B near Le Sars, they engaged four enemy fighters, likely Rolands, at about 10,000 feet, spiralling downwards to 2,000 feet during the fighting. Rankin emptied a drum from his Lewis gun into one of the aircraft, which "was observed to descend steeply and crash in a shell hole."

Previously, on September 1, Rankin was wounded. According to an article in the *Carleton Sentinel*,

> On this day he went out in an observation plane and was attacked by a fast German Fokker, which on account of being able to manoeuvre quickly got their range with his machine gun before the heavier British plane could turn. The pilot was shot through the leg and fainted. Lt. Rankin not knowing why his pilot did not back and turn, tried to swing the machine gun around and

found its moorings had jammed, so it could not be moved. It was then that he received a bullet across his head, fortunately nothing but an ugly graze. Seeing now the predicament of his pilot, Lt. Rankin seized the steering gear to steady the machine until the pilot came to, when they dove into a thick cloud, losing the Fokker and descending safely into the British lines.

Rankin's luck ended on October 23, when he and Barnard were escorting a photo reconnaissance mission over Bapaume. Barnard described the action in dramatic detail in his air combat report.

When escorting a camera machine over Bapaume we attacked one of several HA [hostile aircraft] which were in the neighbourhood of the camera machine....When these had been driven off we turned for home...but found three more HA on our tail.... [Rankin] put one drum into one which was passing straight over our heads at very close range, and this machine immediately became out of control, the tail and back of the fuselage being on fire. It went down in a spin. The remaining two HA were now firing from behind and [Rankin] stood up to get a shot at them...one more HA was seen to go down in a nose dive with smoke from the engine.... [Rankin] was still firing when he was hit in the head and fell sideways over the side of the nacelle. I managed to catch his coat as he was falling, and by getting in the front seat pulled him back. I then got back in the pilot seat. The engine and most of the controls had been shot but I managed to get the machine over our lines and landed 200 yards behind our front line.

After landing, Barnard was rescued by nearby soldiers and taken to a dressing station in the rear. Rankin was buried by the wreckage of the plane, but his grave and marker were soon lost on the shifting battlefield. He is listed among the missing on the Arras Flying Services Memorial, the memorial for those airmen who served on the Western Front and

Arras Flying Services Memorial. Wernervc BY-S 4.0

whose bodies are "missing" — either they were never recovered, could not be identified, or their graves were lost. Several other New Brunswick airmen are found on the memorial, including Talmage Hanning from Fredericton, Stephen Dawson and Clair Gilmour from Saint John, Albert Melanson from South Bathurst, and Lloyd Sands from Moncton.

Captain Percy Byron McNally was killed in action on August 13, 1917. Born in Fredericton on January 21, 1887, the youngest child of Byron and Annie, Percy graduated from the Philadelphia Dental College and several years before the war moved to Alberta, where he became a dentist. He served in the militia's 19th Alberta Dragoons and 101st Regiment (Edmonton Fusiliers). On December 7, 1915, he enlisted in Calgary in the Canadian Army Dental Corps and shortly afterwards went to England where he served as a dentist. Perhaps exercising some literary licence, the *Daily Gleaner* reported, "After spending some months in England with the dental division he became restless, and longed for the field of battle where he could do his part more actively, for his country." On February 28, 1916, he transferred to the CEF's 50th Battalion (Calgary) as a captain and served at the front. On November 18, McNally suffered a superficial shrapnel wound to the face and had to be hospitalized. Afterwards, a medical examination showed he had fallen arches in his feet and was unfit for continued service with the infantry in the trenches. On February 28, 1917, he was seconded to the RFC, and during the spring and early summer underwent training at Reading. He was appointed a flying officer on June 25, and on July 17 joined No. 55 Squadron, a day-bomber squadron, in France, a few days after Jack Hanson was killed.

McNally flew a DH.4; his air gunner was Air Mechanic 2nd Class Cornelius Kelly from Ireland. By then, No. 55 Squadron had been conducting long-distance raids against enemy targets around Ghent, a port city in northwest Belgium, deep inside German-held territory. A powerful 375-horsepower Rolls Royce engine enabled the DH.4 to fly at 133 mph at 10,000 feet, climb to 16,000 feet in about sixteen minutes, and reach a ceiling of 22,000 feet. Carrying two 230-lb or four 112-lb bombs, it could remain aloft for nearly four hours. As such, the DH.4 was the best bomber the RFC had, and superior to the German Gotha.

On August 13, McNally and Kelly took part in a squadron attack on the marshalling yard at Deinze, to the southwest of Ghent. According to an article by Paul Van den Hende and Dirk Praet, during the mission they were attacked by German fighters from Jasta 11, and their bomber was shot down by Leutnant Wilhelm Bockelmann and crashed at Uitbergen, about fifteen miles east of Ghent. The mayor of the town witnessed the action: "I saw a plane fall vertically down in the direction of Uitbergen. It had lost its wings, the propellor was spinning at full speed. When it hit the ground there was a huge flame. A little later we saw the wings drop from the clouds, they spun and fell slowly." A large group of Belgians was kept back from the burning wreck by German soldiers and gendarmes. The fire was extinguished, and the bodies of McNally and Kelly were removed to the town morgue and placed in poplar caskets. Next day, they were buried in the local cemetery by a local pastor with several town officials present. By the following day, the two graves had been decorated with flowers. However, the Germans directed that the airmen should be exhumed and brought to nearby Dendermonde, where a military funeral would be conducted by British prisoners of war. On the fifteenth, the caskets were taken to the municipal cemetery in Dendermonde, where a few local officials, some German soldiers, and twenty to thirty POWs were present at the funeral service conducted by a Protestant chaplain. Percy McNally's grave at the Dendermonde Communal Cemetery and Extension is marked today with a Commonwealth War Graves Commission headstone.

Most combat deaths occurred in 1918. They included that of Lieutenant Arthur Clair Gilmour, who was born in Saint John on May 26, 1893. Before the war, he was a men's clothier and furnisher with three years of service with the 62nd St. John Fusiliers and was married to Nellie Beatrice Williams. On January 20, 1916, he enlisted in the 115th Battalion as a lieutenant, and on July 23 embarked at Halifax for England. Nellie gave birth to a son, Clair, on October 3, three months after Gilmour arrived in Britain. In early December, he was attached to the Garrison Duty Battalion at Bramshott, Hampshire, as part of the musketry staff. Later, he transferred to the 3rd Labour Battalion (later redesignated the 11th Battalion, Canadian Railway Troops), and was second-in-command of one of its companies. On February 9, 1917, he left for France, where, according to an article in the *St. John Standard*, his unit conducted pioneer operations in the vicinity of Ypres previous to the attack on Messines Ridge on June 7. "His company successfully carried out important work and as a result of distinguished conduct Lieutenant Gilmour was recommended for a military cross."

On August 26, Gilmour was attached to the RFC on probation as an observer and returned to England. After completing his training, he was appointed a flying officer (observer) and was again sent to France on November 16, where he joined No. 82 Squadron. He was briefly attached to No. 16 Squadron and then returned to the 82nd. On March 6, 1918, his plane was shot down south of Saint-Quentin and he was listed as missing. It was hoped he had survived and been made a prisoner, until German newspaper sources confirmed his death through the Geneva Red Cross. They also stated that he had been buried at the Itancourt Mézières Cemetery. The Wounded and Missing Department of the Canadian Red Cross Society later followed up with additional details. According to Second Lieutenant J.E. Kernahan of the 82nd Squadron,

[Gilmour] was out on photography between Alincourt and Mezieres. He was observer and the missing Second Lieutenant L.D. Sisley was Pilot. Lieutenant Morton of 82nd squad, who was on another machine in the same formation told me that they were attacked by five Huns, and Lieutenant Gilmour was seen to be hit and to collapse in the cockpit after which the machine was enveloped in flames. He was then seen to come down by an artillery officer on 122nd Siege Battery. He saw the machine come down and fall on its back and burst into flames.

The Red Cross also confirmed that he had been buried in the military hospital cemetery at Itancourt. It is not clear if his grave was found afterwards, but today he is remembered on the Arras Flying Services Memorial.

Many other airmen were lost to the flying services when they were shot down behind enemy lines, captured, and made POWs in Germany for the duration of the hostilities.

New Brunswick Airmen Taken Prisoner of War, by Date Captured

McMillan, Robert Earnshaw, September 19, 1917

Golding, Kenneth Logan, October 24, 1917

Steeves, Gordon Tracy, March 18, 1918

Carter, Albert Desbrisay, May 19, 1918

MacDonald, Donald Angus, May 27, 1918

Cyr, Arthur Joseph, July 20, 1918

Brown, Lee Roy Lowerison, August 8, 1918

Belliveau, Alfred Hilaire, August 27, 1918

Heine, Roland Wallace, September 14, 1918

Cawley, Charles Frederick, September 27, 1918

Chapter Six

Prisoners of War

An unusually large number of Canadian airmen were captured during the Great War when they were shot down behind enemy lines. RFC, RNAS, and RAF officers made up almost a quarter of British officers taken during the war. According to Wise, 377 Canadians became POWs or were interned. At least ten came from New Brunswick. Several of them left in-depth accounts that provide us with informative insight into their experiences.

Shot Down and Captured
The earliest POW from among New Brunswick's airmen was Flight Sub-Lieutenant Robert Earnshaw McMillan. Born at Jacquet River in Restigouche County in November 1894, McMillan graduated from Mount Allison University in 1915, and in March 1916 joined the CEF's 132nd (North Shore) Battalion as a lieutenant, having already undergone military training with the militia's 73rd Northumberland Regiment and Mount Allison's COTC. He sailed with the 132nd to England in October, and on January 19, 1917, entered the RNAS through the Dominion Naval Service. Between February and August, he underwent flight training at Crystal Palace in south London, Vendôme in France, Cranwell, and Dover, and on July 18 was promoted to flight sub-lieutenant and "Recommended

for Scouts." After undertaking active service at the front, according to his air service file, on September 19 McMillan's Sopwith Triplane "was Last seen going down under control NE of St. Julien after [a] fight with enemy scouts." He was later reported as being captured at Messines. He was a POW at Karlsruhe and then Holzminden until December 13, 1918, when he was repatriated to Dover after having been a prisoner in Germany for almost fifteen months.

Another of the earliest New Brunswick airmen to be captured was the RFC's Second Lieutenant Kenneth Logan Golding, who was shot down and taken prisoner on October 24, 1917. Born in Saint John on April 19, 1893, Golding managed a local branch of the Bank of Nova Scotia, then spent time in Prince Edward Island and Toronto, where he was in charge of other branches of the bank. In early 1917, he resigned to join the RFC and underwent three months of training at Camp Borden. In July, he travelled to England, where he received his second lieutenant's commission on July 23. After only three weeks of training, Golding went to France, and on August 14 was posted to No. 81 Squadron and then, on September 29, joined No. 19 Squadron at the front alongside Major Albert Desbrisay Carter. On October 24, Golding was flying a SPAD VII as part of a mission during the Battle of Passchendaele, near Ypres. According to Golding's account quoted by historian Stewart Taylor:

SPAD VII. Wikimedia Commons

We had not been flying over the lines very long when we sighted a large formation of Huns and our leader led us to attack. In the mix-up that followed I saw one of the machines I fired on go down but almost immediately afterwards my gun jammed and I saw that I had been separated from the rest of our formation and Huns all around me. I did what I could to get away, all the while trying to correct my gun, but found the jam was one which could be corrected only on the ground.

In the meantime two Huns were following me. One was just in my rear and I tried to manipulate the machine so as to get away from him and at the same time avoid flying a straight course, but he stuck right with me. I finally shook him off by turning sharply and flying directly at him. I missed him but by a few yards and evidently he did not like this as he immediately dove and I did not see him again.

I was so taken up with this chap that I had not noticed No. 2 who now came down on me like a ton of bricks. I am not sure whether this chap or No. 1 fired a burst which among other things broke my mirror just over my head but No. 2 soon put a burst into my engine piercing some of the cylinders and sending the water up in a cloud of steam. I kept on as best I could as I still had hopes of reaching our side of the lines though the engine was running badly and I knew would soon seize. From then the Hun kept firing intermittently and finally put a burst through the fuselage which cut off my petrol supply.

I switched on the emergency tank but the engine was barely keeping me up. I was slightly wounded in the left arm by the burst which cut off my petrol supply and afterward found from a German Flying Corps officer who was in the hospital with me that three shots had passed through my flying coat.

Shortly afterwards, Golding crashed near a farmhouse behind enemy lines. Germans pulled him out of his machine and transported him by ambulance to a hospital in Lille, where he was X-rayed and his wounds treated, and then placed in a room by himself. The next day, the two German officers who had forced him down visited, and the pilot who received credit for bringing him down informed Golding that he was the pilot's twenty-second victory. After becoming stable Golding was sent to a hospital for prisoners in Tournai, and at the end of the year he went by hospital train to Nuremburg and then the POW camp at Karlsruhe in Baden, a southern province of Germany near the French and Swiss borders. In late April 1918, he was exchanged for captured German officers and interned in Holland. On August 18, 1918, he was repatriated to Britain.

Major Albert Desbrisay Carter, New Brunswick's greatest ace, flying with No. 19 Squadron, was brought down and taken prisoner at La Bassée on May 19, 1918. According to Carter's friend from Saint John, Captain Stuart Bell, "the day Carter was taken prisoner he engaged with an enemy plane…but his machine gun failed to function properly and he shot off his own propellor, forcing him to come down, and as he was hunting within enemy lines he was taken prisoner." He was officially reported as a prisoner at Karlsruhe on July 12 and then at Landshut, in Bavaria, on August 8.

Carter was able to remain in contact with family through letters and telegrams organized by the International Committee of the Red Cross. His family learned more about his capture when Mrs. Charles Scott, his sister in Amherst, Nova Scotia, received a telegram on June 15, 1918, stating: "Prisoner Karlsruhe send parcels food chocolate weekly. Desbrisay." It was passed on to the Carters at nearby Point de Bute.

Stuart Bell also related that Carter's description of the way British officers were treated in the German prison camps "would make the blood run cold."

On one occasion he as senior British officer went to the commandant of the camp and protested, demanding that they be treated as British officers and according to the Hague convention. To this the German replied, "I will give you to understand that you are in Germany and you will do damned well as we tell you to." Major Carter's reply to this was, "Yes, and that is the reason why the whole world is fighting you, you have no sense of honor or respect for conventions." For this he received three days bread and water and cells.

Carter was transferred to Danzig, and on December 13, 1918, was repatriated to Leith, Scotland. When Bell saw him two days after his arrival in England, he found that Carter had lost thirty pounds during his confinement.

Lieutenant Donald Angus MacDonald became a POW in late May 1918. Born in Saint John on October 19, 1893, he received a Bachelor of Science in forest engineering from the University of New Brunswick and found work in Ottawa with the Canadian government, doing reconnaissance and surveying for the Department of the Interior. MacDonald was living in Kamloops, British Columbia, when, on May 1, 1917, he enlisted as a lieutenant in the Canadian Forestry Corps and proceeded overseas. On September 19, he was seconded to the RFC and after training in England was appointed a flying officer on February 12, 1918. He joined No. 99 Squadron at the front in mid-April.

On May 27, MacDonald and his observer were shot down while flying a DH.9. He summed up the mission in his diary, held at the Directorate of History in Ottawa: "Left ground at 10 am for raid on Bensdorf. Met 5 Huns. Only 4 in our formation & I was out of luck for a position. Got out of formation after dropping bombs & had my tail plane shot off on left side. Loop & spin. Three Huns bit the dust. Landed one mile from lines. Oh! What a feeling. For duration now!"

MacDonald's comrades learned of his fate when the Germans flew over the British lines and dropped a note stating that he and his observer had made a successful landing uninjured fifteen miles behind their lines due to an engine failure. He was taken to local German headquarters and then sent to Saint-Avold, east of Metz near the German border, where he walked five miles in flying boots to a POW camp. After being questioned by a German officer, he was sent to a hotel in Karlsruhe, where he stayed for several days. He described it as an "awful place" and found his confinement "aggravating." On June 4, MacDonald went to the prison camp where he roomed with several other officers and filled out Red Cross papers.

On June 13, 1918, MacDonald left by train with thirty prisoners for the POW camp at Landshut. Guarded by only one officer and eight soldiers, five POW officers escaped along the way. Once the remainder arrived, MacDonald moved into a room in a hut that he described as a "quiet place." He began making living arrangements, sending a card to the Bank of Montreal to pay for parcels of Swiss and Danish bread, and wired home to "hurry parcels." He received weekly mess bills for expenses, one of which totalled 150 German marks, which he described as an "Outrageous expenditure for trifles." Most days he played rummy, bridge, and poker for money. He also wrote or wired home often. Frequent rain during mid-June and throughout July led him to lament, "Oh to be back at my [squadron]."

These prisoners sometimes met friends and acquaintances at the camps, especially among newly arriving prisoners. Even though the number of New Brunswick POWs was relatively small, they seemed to encounter one another frequently. While at Landshut, Albert D. Carter joined MacDonald in his hut when he arrived on June 28.

On July 15, MacDonald was moved from Landshut to Stralsund Camp for officers on the Baltic Sea coast. During the trip, he was impressed with the countryside—on the way to Berlin, they "[p]assed through wonderful crops & forest. Many factories in the district." Leipzig was a "[b]eautiful place & [had a] fine station." By the time he arrived at Stralsund, five hundred officers were already there, but his group were the first "flys" to arrive. He described it as a "[p]retty spot" but the "[g]rub [was] poor."

Some of the prisoners' food was issued at the camps, but they also received food parcels, either from home or outside agencies such as the Red Cross and the RAF, or paid for food themselves. From the camp, they received biscuits and bread, sometimes in large quantities that was shared among several prisoners. They also got jam, sugar, sardines, and salmon from outside sources. From home MacDonald received cigarettes. Occasionally, the parcels arrived at the camp "fairly well smashed up" and completely rifled. These parcels became much anticipated. In his diary, MacDonald noted their arrivals and contents. (By November 9, he had received forty-two parcels.) Outside agencies also provided these POWs with assistance, especially the Red Cross and the Bureau de secours de Berne pour les prisonniers de guerre, in Switzerland. Nevertheless, hunger was a persistent problem. MacDonald noted food shortages in his diary on several occasions: "Awfully hungry. Beans tomorrow"; "Meals getting damned small"; and on July 23, "Hungry to-day, faint & weak for food."

Perhaps not surprisingly, prisoners suffered from health problems. MacDonald had "face pimples" and toothaches for which he saw a camp doctor and dentist. He also noted ongoing unspecified health problems: "Feeling rotten, sore," headaches, and feeling sick to his stomach, which caused him to be "sick in bed — rough trip" and needing to see the camp doctor.

They also suffered psychological distress, especially boredom, where each day was "same as other." MacDonald became homesick as time passed, writing, "Oh to be home. How long have I to stay in Germany," and "Oh to be home in Canada!" Occasionally, friction arose among the prisoners, leading them to form separate messes from the others. MacDonald also experienced frustration with family at home, perhaps as a result of his growing awareness of how things had changed for him, whereas family seemed to stay the same. In early October 1918, he began receiving packages and letters from a Marion, possibly his sister, noting early on, "God bless her — I wonder what she thinks" and "the darling." By mid-November, however, his tone had changed. On November 13, he wrote: "Letter from Marion. How maddening! How self satisfied she appears. Fearfully upset over such a letter. What is the matter with her or is it me? I don't know how I shall take her when I go back....What do I want to do back in Can." The next day, he received two more letters from her. "Ouch!...M will not change I think!"

To relieve their boredom, the prisoners engaged in various pastimes, including sports—hockey in the winter and rugger and football during the warmer weather—but poor physical conditioning sometimes made sports difficult. After playing football, MacDonald noted: "Old knee is still bad" and the next day "lame and knocked up." At Stralsund camp, MacDonald attended band concerts at a theatre put on by other ranks and studied German — "might as well learn it."

Another captured New Brunswick airmen was Lieutenant Arthur Joseph Cyr of Saint-Hilaire in Madawaska County. Born on June 15, 1891, Cyr enlisted in the 165th (Acadian) Battalion shortly after graduating from law school. After his pilot training, he joined No. 46 Squadron in France, and was shot down near Armentières. According to Alfred Belliveau's diary, Cyr later told him that he had been flying at the front for only a week when, during a bombing raid on July 20, 1918, he was straggling behind his comrades with a "balky" engine and "was jumped by three Fokkers and an Albatross, who shot him pretty well to bits, and he crashed most emphatically." Cyr's father, Honoré, living at Upper Pokemouche in Gloucester County, was notified on September 11 via telegram from the Red Cross: "Prisoner Rastatt." Cyr and Belliveau spent a few weeks together in Rastatt prison camp, near Karlsruhe, but then were separated. On October 19, Cyr was transferred to a camp at Ingolstadt, in upper Bavaria.

As for conditions in the camps, in an account published by the *North Shore Leader* in February 1919, Cyr stated that he was "kept hungry being given one half pound of black bread per day and mangled soup every four days. Bran was another food commodity and the only drink was barley soup flavored with meat." He also stated that, while a prisoner, he was "used fairly" by the Germans — as officers, they were given no duties. Most German camp officers were "haughty in manner and most overbearing in demeanor, [and] jostled him about." An exception was an officer who had spent five years in Canada as a music professor at McGill University before returning to Germany in 1912. "His training in Canada must have civilized him, as he was exceptionally kind and generous to me." When Cyr needed any little commodity, this officer tried to find it for him "and make life worth living." Of the rest, "he had nothing to relate but brutality and barbarism, and pitied the poor lads in the ranks who were wantonly made slaves in the commercial interests of an unscrupulous foe as Germany."

One of the last New Brunswickers to be captured was Roland Wallace Heine. His experiences as a POW are described in much detail in his diary, held at the Provincial Archives of New Brunswick, through a long letter he wrote after the Armistice at Königsberg, in East Prussia, that was printed in the *Moncton Daily Times* on January 6, 1919, and in the transcript of an in-depth interview he gave to the *Moncton Transcript* and subsequently published in various provincial newspapers. The latter two sources offer a franker description of his exploits than does the diary, which is clearly quite circumspect.

Heine was born on April 12, 1894, and was an insurance manager living in Moncton when he joined the RNAS on January 7, 1918, through the Dominion Naval Service and underwent training at Greenwich and Cranwell. By September, he was a pilot with the Independent Force's No. 216 Squadron, RAF, flying Handley-Page 0/100 twin-engine, night bombers from Nancy, France. The Handley-Page had become the mainstay of the strategic bomber offensive against Germany. Powered by two

Handley-Page 0/100 bomber. LAC-3194166

250-horsepower engines, it could carry ten 112-lb bombs on long-range missions (up to nine-and-half hours) or fourteen bombs on shorter sorties. On the night of September 14, 1918, Heine's plane was detailed to bomb an aerodrome in Alsace-Lorraine. At 8:30 p.m. he left the airfield with his observer, Lieutenant Jewett of the US Army Air Service and a gun layer, and successfully carried out their "show" (the Handley-Page carried a crew of four, but Heine mentions only these three). During their return to the southwest of Metz, miles behind enemy lines, they were "archied like H---" by German anti-aircraft guns. All of a sudden, his engines "cocked up" at about 4,500 feet. He did his best to glide toward the lines, but seeing it was impossible, he picked out a field on which to land. All the time, they were "given a warm reception" by enemy machine guns from the ground, and he was shot through the wrist and cut under the chin by shrapnel, leaving him with only one hand to pilot the bomber. The ground was uneven and the machine went over on its nose, but no one was hurt. Once down, they took their bearings, and as they were only about four miles from the front lines, decided to try to escape. They set fire to their plane and picked their way forward very carefully for about two hours. By around 10 p.m., when they were about three kilometres from the German lines, several machine guns opened fire on them without warning, and they fell onto their stomachs, where they lay for about twenty minutes. They heard voices all around them and about a hundred Germans closed in on them using whistles to coordinate their movements. "Realizing we could not get under cover, we 'gave up.'" When they were finally taken at about 2 a.m., the Germans "were rather kind to us."

> They insisted upon carrying me to the main road, where they made me comfortable by means of coats, etc. sending in the meantime for hot coffee and water. In a short time we were picked up by a transport and taken to headquarters of some kind where a sergeant dressed my wound by merely putting iodine and a bandage upon it. We were directly sent to another H.Q. and there I was given a bed to rest upon and told I should leave again at 5 a.m.

They walked to a small train station under escort of two guards, "who I may mention were fully 'fed up' with the war, and as a consequence were very lenient with us."

At around 8 a.m. they arrived by train at Metz. where there was great excitement, the town having been bombed the night before for the third consecutive night. Hundreds of women and children had taken shelter at the Metz railway station, and some were hostile toward the airmen: "[H]ad we not the protection of our guards I am confident our position would have been precarious." They boarded another train, destination unknown. So far, they had received nothing to eat until "a small boy (well dressed) gave us each two biscuits which was very much appreciated."

Several hours later they arrived at Saint-Avold, to the east of Metz near the German border. They walked to a camp, where Heine became separated from his observer and gun layer, who were put in cells while he went into hospital, where he remained for six days. He was also interrogated by a German officer who spoke fluent English. He was very kind, offering cigarettes and a drink, and began a general conversation trying to get information from Heine. Later, they were joined by an observer from the German air force who wanted to know where Heine's aerodrome was so they could drop a note about his capture. Heine's comment on these methods was: "I would not trust any German the length of his nose, and I told him so. He got very nasty and left the room. I may say I have had in all about five interrogations at different places and am glad to say they do not even know my squadron number."

Conditions at the hospital were poor. Food was scarce—he received only a bowl of soup for the day and it was very bad. It was nonetheless the same food as German officers and soldiers received at this point in the war. Medical treatment was also lacking. The hospital was very unclean, and the staff dressed his wounds when they felt like it. He noted that, "had I not stolen some paper bandages and kept my own wound clean, I may have had serious trouble." Life in the hospital was generally "tiresome": he couldn't leave, and he was guarded like a "criminal." On September 18, all of the other officer prisoners were moved to another hospital, leaving him by himself. The only bright spot was a female night nurse — a "queen" — whose brother was a POW in England, where he was treated well, and she felt it was her duty to do the same for the English prisoners. Heine received many favours from her, including cigarettes, sugar candy, and rice pudding. He wrote that he "will long remember her thoughtfulness."

The condition of other prisoners who entered the hospital, however, were much worse: "our men come to the hospital so thin that every bone on their body could be seen. These men had been working 'behind the lines' from daylight till dark on three bowls of watery soup per day. They were not put in barracks at night, and I am told many died from exposure. Also at this hospital I have seen our men come in from the salt mines with the flesh hanging from their bodies. The treatment in these mines is simply indescribable." He also reported how, at the stables at Saint-Avold, some men fed on the food that was given to the horses.

These experiences shaped Heine's attitudes toward the Germans. He came to believe they should be severely punished for their conduct. "The only people whom we have a right to feel sorry for are the wee small children and the aged women. Otherwise I would like to see every other German man and woman suffer as a consequence of this war."

On September 20, conditions suddenly improved when the kaiser visited the hospital: Heine's room was cleaned and washed, and fresh linen was put on his bed. He watched the event through his window. "On account of the feeling in Alsace and Lorraine" toward the Germans, a large guard was formed outside the hospital. All the men who were able to walk formed up in the square, where a review took place. The kaiser talked with his troops, assuring them that the war would soon end. "The thing that surprised me most was no cheering whatever took place during the review or on his departure. This shows how the feeling was and the spirit of his men at this time."

The next day, Heine was driven for two hours by car to Mörchingen, accompanied by a doctor. There he was placed with other British officers and treated well. His wounds were dressed daily and by then he was able rise each day. He assisted a nurse in dressing the wounds of his fellow prisoners and German soldiers. Then, on October 5, he was sent to Karlsruhe, a distributing camp all fliers went through before being sent to a permanent camp. He travelled second class by train, where he met German officers, one of whom spoke English and told Heine that the war would be over soon, which gave him "great hopes." Along the way, they passed through very clean and neat German towns and villages that "the people had every reason to be proud of." Nevertheless, they were poorly dressed and wore "fed up" expressions on their faces.

Once he arrived at Karlsruhe, he was placed in a hotel for three days, where he was poorly fed, receiving breakfast consisting of coffee made from burnt barley and acorns, and soup for dinner and supper. He also received three slices of bread made from potato peelings, corn meal, and several other meals good for about a week.

He underwent another interrogation, during which the German intelligence officer told him the war would be over soon and was sorry he could not treat them the way their officers were in England. He also told Heine the German people received very limited food — one egg per week per head and seven ounces of horse meat per week — and conditions were almost enough to cause a revolution.

On October 8, Heine and four other officers were marched through town to the main camp, located in a square and consisting of huts enclosed by fences. Upon arrival, they were stripped and searched from head to toe, then given a bed. They were allowed to walk where they chose and, according to Heine, "this privilege was grand after having been 'shut up' so much since my being captured." Twice a week, the British Red Cross issued food to the prisoners, including biscuits, tea, cheese, pressed beef, and dripping. The Germans also had a canteen where the prisoners could buy various articles, such as cigars, cigarettes, soap, canned meat, bread, and butter, all at high prices.

On October 12, 1918, he wrote in his diary: "during my moments of leisure since being captured I naturally have thought much about 'My Wife,' and if I only knew she knew I was safe and well, life would certainly have a brighter aspect, and I would be more contented." At Karlsruhe, Heine was able to correspond with Winnifred once a week using a postcard or *Kriegsgefangen* (POW) letter provided by the camp and reviewed by a censor. In these, he described his circumstances and offered her comfort. On October 9, he wrote:

> I am now perfectly well, and quite happy considering everything. Have been treated fine since being captured, and with food from "Red Cross" have not suffered so far. The German food is very good considering, so I hope you will "cheer up" and realize we shall some day be united, whereas before this was an uncertainty... and remember every road must have a turning.

In a letter on the fourteenth, he continued in the same way, writing

> I dreamt last night I was home with you, and oh, the agony when I realized it was not true: but cheer up, and the "good times" will come again. The camp [here] is quite comfortable, and I do much reading & studying. The other officers are very nice in my room, and we have great amusement cooking. I will show you "some dishes" at Loch Lomond when we go there on our second honey-moon? Your lonesome, but true and happy Boy, Roland.

On October 24, Heine and about thirty other POWs left for another camp in Bavaria, travelling through countryside consisting of well-kept farms and forests. They passed through Munich, the capital of Bavaria, on their way to Landshut two hours on, where Heine noted its beautiful setting in the Isar River valley. The POWs arrived at a sanitary camp, where they received inoculations and vaccinations. The prisoners bought food from a restaurant, paying about $1.25 a day, which got them enough to be satisfied, including coffee and bread for breakfast, potatoes and cabbage for lunch, and potatoes and soup for dinner. They also received meat once a week and butter once every four weeks.

Daily Life in the Camps

Lieutenant Alfred Belliveau from Fredericton was among the later POWs. On August 27, 1918, Belliveau failed to return from a mission and was listed as missing. Alfred's family received official notification from the government in Ottawa, and a short time later a letter arrived from a fellow officer, which was published in the *Daily Gleaner*. The officer was unable to tell them what had happened, only that "he was last seen on the other side of the lines among the other machines of the same patrol, but there were clouds about, also they had a pretty tight scrap soon after that.... Anyway frankly there is nothing to indicate in the least what his fate is." In early October, after several weeks of anxious waiting for news, his father received a telegram from the Red Cross stating that Alfred was a prisoner at Rastatt.

During his four months of confinement in Germany, Belliveau kept a diary of his experiences that today is found at the Centre d'études acadiennes Anselme-Chiasson at the Université de Moncton. Throughout his captivity, he kept it hidden in different places to "baffle the prison camp censors." In the hope of avoiding confiscation in the event of discovery, he purposely refrained from including derogatory information about the Germans, including the use of "Hun." He states the text was not tampered with by the Germans, suggesting that they read it but let it pass inspection. The diary provides a detailed description of his daily life as a POW.

Lieutenant Alfred Belliveau in his flying uniform. P37-A016, Centre d'études acadiennes Anselme-Chiasson, Université de Moncton

During a balloon "busting" mission on August 27, Belliveau was shot down behind German lines and captured near Étaing, to the east of Arras. Shortly afterwards, he was taken to Douai, where he was held with several other officers, including a couple of American aviators he knew from Dover. He was well treated by a German officer who spoke flawless English he had learned while living in the United States and who gave Belliveau a book to read. Nevertheless, he suspected the German was an intelligence officer. He quickly discovered how awful the food was, but with the money in his pocket he was able to buy some French cigarettes and soap—which were also awful. Fortunately, he was able to pick some mulberries from a tree in the garden next to where he was being held.

On August 30, Belliveau and several other prisoners were taken by train to Valenciennes, and then marched to the town of Saint-André, near the Belgian border. There they were warmly greeted by French civilians, who gave them food. They were confined in a large prison and helped by other prisoners who were already receiving Red Cross parcels. Most of the other prisoners were English, but there were also some French and Italians, even a few Russians. They were given the freedom of the building and yard, and French women who spoke to them through the windows bribed the guards at the gate and sent in food. According to Belliveau, "we dined like royalty in their castle."

The prisoners spent much of their time hunting the vermin that infested their clothes and beds, cracking them between their thumbnails. Within the officers' mess, they formed a "family circle" that pooled their food. The women of the town formed a Red Cross Committee and sent in soup, bread, and other items. They had a corporal who heated the water, made tea and cocoa, and washed up afterwards. The officers played bridge and chess. Belliveau wrote that "we were reasonably content with our lot for the time being considering everything."

On September 3, 1918, Belliveau was among twenty-four officers, including nine airmen (five Americans, three Englishmen, and one Canadian) who left for Karlsruhe. It was difficult finding enough food for all of them; the French sent them a good breakfast, plus bread, cocoa, and tinned goods for their journey, as well as soap, "which we were badly in need of." After marching to Avesnes, near the Belgian border, they travelled by train to Brussels, then on into Germany, arriving in Karlsruhe at noon on the fifth. They then went on to Rastatt, where they finished their fifty-eight-hour journey. Rastatt, a distribution centre for captured Allied officers, was located inside an ancient fortress. According to Belliveau, it was "a fairly nice place, with gardens and plenty of room. And what was even better there were baths, a canteen, a library, a barber shop, and even a tailor!" The prison population consisted of about a hundred English and American officers, as well as thirty French and a dozen Italians. Among them was Belliveau's comrade from the 165th Battalion, Lieutenant Arthur Cyr, who had been captured in July. A "fair number" of orderlies were also present.

The prisoners were provided with many amenities, including mail service that allowed them to send several cards and a few letters each month. They also received as much mail as people back home wanted to send. In letters to family, Belliveau was circumspect in what he told them. As he wrote in his diary, "it's better not to tell them too much. Let me do the worrying! I can worry for all of us!" He was also able to receive money by writing an IOU that he paid off with funds forwarded by his bank in London. With £10 he received 210 German marks, which he used to purchase apples in the canteen, among other things. He wrote enthusiastically that, "with good credit, backed up with solid liquid assets, you are master of all you survey!"

Prisoners could also read books from the library and attend chapel on Sundays, where a German priest said Mass and gave a sermon in English. Belliveau found comfort in religion: "I guess we all need a religion of some sort to turn to more than we realize, sometimes." He also met an English priest, who conducted missions around the various prison camps. "He gathered the small flocks of catholics around him, and we had an interesting talk." Belliveau also attended language classes in French and German at the library. "It is a good way to utilize the time, and I think I may have a gift for language." Belliveau began exercising every day "to get hardened up a bit," using gymnastics equipment, such as the horizontal bar, that was familiar to him from his time as a physical instructor.

At Rastatt, as in other camps, food became the prisoners' chief pre-occupation, and they "plunged once more into the gentle art or science of cookery." Becoming their own cooks, they experimented with different combinations of German bread, biscuits, tinned meat, and jam, which they took down to the kitchen and cooked as a meat pie, fish cake, jam tart, or "some nameless thing." They "clubbed together" in fours or fives to pool their food, and took turns as chef for the day. Some turned out to be good at it and did much of the cooking, while the rest served as helpers or assistants. Belliveau wrote that cooking "gives us something to do and keeps us from brooding."

Periodically, they received food parcels from the Red Cross and biscuits, but they got little from the Germans, the camp diet consisting mostly of carrots, cabbage, and bread. So they were hungry much of the time, despite complaints to their captors. Belliveau recorded on September 24 that they had finally received an adequate food supply:

> Loud cheers! We were rounded out of bed this morning by some real food from the camp, the first we've seen for a week. There was a supply of bread biscuits, about six tins of meat fish, and paste, emptied out on a big dish, plus a bit of jam, a bit of cheese, and a bit of pudding. In our glee we did a war dance for about ten minutes, in celebration.... The German soup is not very nourishing at best, and no matter how much of it you eat, you are still hungry. Personally, I feel just about starved, and I could have eaten it all. But we restrained ourselves, and by careful management, made it last for lunch, tea, and dinner.

Lice were also an ongoing problem. Periodically, the prisoners were paraded to a barracks where their bedding and clothing were cleaned in a steam chamber, and they had baths while they waited.

The POWs received up-to-date news of the war from newly arriving prisoners, much of which, by September 1918, was "encouraging." They learned of the successful attacks against the Hindenburg Line and the elimination of the Saint-Mihiel Salient. Nevertheless, rumours abounded, especially about the course of the war and where they were going next. "Rumors seem to be developing into a pastime, like cards," Belliveau wrote.

The war was brought close to home by air raids on Karlsruhe and Rastatt in September. On the twentieth, he wrote: "We had two air raids last night [on Karlsruhe], both of which we enjoyed very much! It was quite an experience to hear the people scampering along the streets, heading for the dugouts which had been prepared in advance. They have a very good artillery barrage here, so good in fact, that we could not tell whether any bombs fell or not."

On September 17, Belliveau began what he later described as "another lap in [our] wanderings through Germany," when twenty-five POWs comprising the English, American, and French fliers were sent from Rastatt to Karlsruhe, where they were held until being sent to a permanent camp. By then, the distribution camp at Rastatt had become overcrowded, as the prisoners could not be shipped elsewhere fast enough to make room for the new arrivals. On September 25, Belliveau was among fifty English, American, Canadian, and French aviators sent to Landshut, where they were held for several days in a quarantine camp. There, they received a series of vaccinations. Belliveau described their temporary home as "a pretty dismal dump with no smokes and nothing to do." They did get fairly good food brought in from a nearby restaurant for 4 marks a day, but no parcels. Their boots were taken to prevent escape, and they wore *Kriegsgefangener* uniforms, which made Belliveau feel like a prisoner. He slept most of the time in this "cheerless" existence and had little interest in exercise, feeling "a bit in the dumps over conditions." Later, they got their clothes back and received some bread biscuits. He also found some old friends when Lieutenant Cyr rejoined them and he met two comrades from No. 54 Squadron who had been shot down in June and August.

On October 4, he was moved to the main camp, where they got tobacco and sugar rations. Belliveau confessed that, although he was not much of a smoker, he did suffer from a lack of sweets. There, he met another fellow New Brunswicker, Major Albert Desbrisay Carter, an "old Mount Allison College man.... He knows Fredericton, my home town there, very well."

Carter, who was a member of the camp committee, became a good friend to Belliveau. "He gets the papers every day, and keeps me posted....I also get his loaf of German bread every issue, since he gets his parcels regularly, and needs very little bread. It may not seem so much to him, but it means a whole lot to me." Belliveau passed on his good fortune to his fellow prisoners. "The Major's German issue bread saved me considerable hunger, but not everyone has an important friend on their side. I help others too at times, if they are in a bad squeeze."

By then, rumours were spreading about Germany's declining war effort. On October 6, they heard that the Germans had sent a peace offer to US President Woodrow Wilson and that German ally Bulgaria had surrendered. Despite the knowledge that the war was coming to an end, the prisoners' monotony was unrelenting. "The time is still passing slowly. All we do besides cooking is reading, playing cards, and walking around the yard. I do quite a bit of walking everyday."

On October 22, Belliveau was moved again, this time to Ingolstadt, in Bavaria, where they got back their boots since escape was unlikely: "Fat chance of our trying anything so foolish, in the middle of Bavaria, with no maps and no money!" The camp was in an old fort and had six or seven prisoners to a room. It also had a canteen where they were able to buy cigarettes and wine. Although there was not much room for walking, it did have an open-air gymnasium and tennis court, although there was no tennis equipment. It also had a French library. "So now, what with reading, walking, and taking exercise in the gymnasium, not to mention preparing our meals, time passes quite quickly, much faster in fact that I would ever have expected." Roll call was not until 9:30 a.m., so they stayed in bed later, which made the day seem shorter. The camp also had a small theatre where the prisoners' troupe, called "The What Nots," put on concerts.

The Armistice and Repatriation

The final stage of the POWs' story was repatriation to Britain and then home. When the Armistice came, they experienced the end of the war in different ways. By late September, Angus MacDonald began hearing news about the course of the war — "Big advance in Palestine," the fall of Saint-Quentin, the burning of Cambrai, and the capture of Lille. Then, on November 7, news of an impending armistice became known, raising their hopes and frustrations. On the ninth, MacDonald wrote in his diary: "Damn the armistice when is it ever going to be signed," and on the next day, "Rumors — Rumors. Riot in Stralsund last night. Armistice is signed — perhaps?" Then, on November 11, the long-awaited news arrived. "Great silent excitement, Kommandant abdicated this a.m. Armistice signed.... We may have trouble yet. I hope we may get home safely soon. We met Kommandant in civies. He laughed & raised his hat. A wonderful change in a short time."

On November 19, an Allied destroyer came into the harbour at Stralsund, causing great excitement. Repatriation was some time off, however, and conditions became more tense. MacDonald soon began showing signs of frustration at not being sent back to Britain. On November 29, he wrote: "are we away from Germany yet? NO!" The wait was made harder by worsening conditions for the German population. On November 25, he noted that "Many 'Huns' around camp begging. 3 loads of Red Cross food for people of Stralsund looted." And, by December 5: "Wrangle to-day re food parcels. Trouble brewing. Grub short. Stralsund to-day. Oh! Was ever such hunger. What a terrible thing war is for the poor women and children. Didn't see a woman & child with a clear eye. Children numerous. Anemia and rickets prevailing. No food in shops. Mob of children beg for tickets." By the tenth he was "Fed up to teeth." Then, on the fifteenth, he sailed to Copenhagen. "Wonderful. Danes all absolutely wonderful. Oh! God be praised & I ungrateful sinner. Love him & thank him from the bottom of my heart!"

On December 31 he was repatriated to England, arriving at Hull, in Yorkshire. He received eight weeks leave, and then was released by the RAF and rejoined the Canadian military forces overseas. MacDonald finally arrived back in Canada in July 1919.

In Bavaria, Roland Heine got his first intimation of the approaching Armistice on November 8, when the camp *Kommandant* called them out and gave a speech. On November 21, now freed, they left the camp, accompanied by Major Albert Carter, for Königsberg, on the Baltic, and eventual repatriation. Travelling by train for four days, they passed through Chemnitz, Dresden, and then Berlin. They now had certain privileges, including their parole, allowing Heine to visit Berlin, which impressed him. On arrival at Königsberg, they were moved to a camp at nearby Pillau, where they stayed for three weeks awaiting transport back to Britain. Ironically, this was Heine's hardest time as a prisoner. He received only one bowl of soup per day. "Many officers became so weak at this camp they were obliged to remain in bed all day in order that they might be able to stand the journey…to Danzig."

At Danzig, they were met by two British cruisers and a German ship flying the British flag. Four hundred and fifty prisoners embarked "amid great excitement" at 6:30 a.m. and an hour later breakfast was served.

> When we entered the magnificent dining room of this boat, seeing white table cloths, real dishes, knives and forks, heaps of bread, bowls of eggs, sardines and all the good things we had thought of for months past, one might imagine the joy and good feeling which came over those officers. Many officers were so touched that handkerchiefs were used frequently.

Over the next four days they sailed for Britain, stopping at Copenhagen, crossing the North Sea, and arriving at Leith, in Scotland.

Alfred Belliveau was repatriated via a different route. Once the Armistice took effect on November 11, food became more plentiful, although camp routine at Landshut carried on. On November 20, Belliveau finally began his return to Britain, being moved to a nearby fort. Over time, they received greater liberty, and were allowed to walk through the countryside and attend Mass in a nearby chapel. "It made us feel pretty good, to have our freedom of religion restored." By mid-December, they able to come and go as they pleased, and they exchanged clothing and other things with the local citizens in exchange for chickens and eggs. Nevertheless, they became "fed up" with delays, and some prisoners planned to leave on their own.

In time, they heard they would be repatriated via Switzerland. On December 17, they were moved by rail along the north shore of Lake Geneva, past the city of Geneva, and into France, where they took a train to Calais. There they boarded a cross-Channel ferry to Dover, arriving on the afternoon of the twenty-fourth after an eight-day trip. After being deloused with hot steam baths for themselves and their clothes, they were sent to London by train and put up in a hotel. After a two-day wait for their luggage to arrive, they discarded their "old rags" and put on their uniforms, "which made us look, as well as feel, like respectable human beings."

Belliveau once again met his old comrade, Arthur Cyr, who had just arrived from the POW camp near Königsberg. Since they were still attached to the RAF rather than a Canadian unit, getting home to Canada required some extra planning, but, via the black market, Cyr was able to book them passage on a good ship due to sail in three weeks. During their wait, they ate at the "better" restaurants and went to the "better" shows in London, including the Grand Opera. After arriving in Halifax, they again went their separate ways, with Belliveau heading straight home to Fredericton. On April 13, 1919, he ceased to be seconded to the Royal Air Force and was discharged shortly afterwards.

Lieutenant Alvah Good reading in No. 35 Squadron's mess at Savy-Bretelle, France. MC 300/MS 69/23, PANB

Chapter Seven

Life behind the Lines and on the Home Front

Unlike infantrymen and other ground troops, Great War airmen were not as continuously engaged in combat operations. Lulls occurred when weather interrupted flying, and the pace of operations slowed when fighting slackened. As a result, airmen tended to have more free time, which they filled in many ways, ranging from leisurely activities around the aerodromes and elsewhere to leave and furloughs in France and Britain as well as in Canada. These latter visits kept them in close contact with their families and friends on the home front.

Life behind the Lines

Life behind the lines varied depending on location and period of the war. Early on, most British airfields in France and Belgium were largely free of direct German attack. Later, however, airmen had to contend with enemy air raids. While Leonard Richardson's No. 74 Squadron was stationed at Clairmarais, near Saint-Omer, they were well withing range of German bombers. On May 18, 1918, a heavy raid by Gothas took place nearby. "They hit the big ammunition dump at Arque just outside St. Omer. We watched the fireworks for an hour. Our 'Archie' opened up but no luck." Because of the threat from these raids the airmen sometimes evacuated their camp at night, either sleeping in a nearby chateau or under trees on camp beds.

Many air officers had base duties other than flying. For example, they took turns as the squadron's duty or orderly officer, often reluctantly. In July 1916, Flight Sub-Lieutenant Lloyd Sands wrote in a letter home about being Duty Officer Standby. "It keeps me here practically all day. Can't go to church or anything else. It is a rainy day and Sunday, so my duties are light, but still I'm here. You should see me with an R.N.A.S. sword-belt [badge of office] dangling under my coat-tail. I look like a tethered dog or an ass with a dangling halter." While undergoing training at Chattis Hill, near Andover, England, Leonard Richardson found this role "bloody awful." Among other things, he inspected the men's mess, guardroom, canteens, and the hangars before lights out and in the morning. While on duty, he slept at headquarters overnight on a wooden bench. Seeing what the men ate and how made him thankful he was an officer. "Well after seeing the way the men, (mechanics) live today, I've come to the conclusion that I'm a poor sport to raise any howl at all, just because everything isn't like it was in Canada." Indeed, flying officers enjoyed many privileges. Among other things they had batmen who looked after many of their needs. Richardson's batman brought him hot water, made fires in his room, shone his boots and belts, and did "other little things." Richardson gave him a shilling once in a while "by way of appreciation."

They also had much time off. RNAS pilot Weldon Carter wrote that

> a pilot's life in France is a comparatively lazy one. In times
> there is "no war on" he does two offensive patrols a day of two
> hours each on fighting planes—a bomber does one raid, which
> will probably take him three hours. When there is a "war on,"
> however, things assume a different attitude."

He also wrote,

> needless to say a flying officer has a good deal of spare time
> on his hands between flights. We do not find such time hard

to use to good advantage. A squadron has ample means of transportation and sometimes we go to see our friends who fight on the ground; or perhaps will play tennis, or cards, and, although most of us in the squadron were Canadians, we have really enjoyed a game of cricket—not a bad game, you know—when one has plenty of time.

They usually had their evenings to themselves, as well.

Then, there were the "dud" days when operations were cancelled, usually due to inclement weather or mechanical problems with their aircraft. As Carter wrote, "these are the days of real sport." Often, they drove to the nearest French or Belgian town of any size and "proceed to paint it red to the best of our ability."

As with most Canadian servicemen during the war, airmen kept close ties with home, updating their families through their letters recounting details of their daily experiences. In a letter published in the *Moncton Daily Times* in August 1917, Observer Jack Hanson of Fredericton wrote at some length to his parents on July 13 about life in No. 55 Squadron in France.

Dear parents:
Well, my first show is over. I think it was Wednesday that we performed. We did not see any signs of a Hun machine. Except for Archie there might not have been a war at all. I'm due for another one today. Cooke, my Canadian friend, who joined the squadron a fortnight after I did, has five shows to his credit. I'm beginning to fear that he will get his wing [observer's badge] before I do. However, mine is bound to come through before long.

The weather has turned fine and warm again. I had to get up at 8 o'clock this morning because the sun was so hot. Just now the tent is rolled up so I am getting the benefit of a lovely breeze. All I wore yesterday was a pair of shorts and a shirt. If we go on the show this afternoon I shall be so warmly clad as to nearly suffocate until we get up into the air. It is some contrast. I find it rather difficult to keep my hands warm. As you can imagine, stiff, cold fingers would be an awful nuisance, so I alternately sit on my hands and beat them together. Some of these days I will find the right rig to keep warm and then I will be Jake. Today I shall wear my finger mittens under my gauntlets.

There are some tanks in the neighbourhood for manoeuvres, so I want to try and set an eye on them. I would not mind having a ride in one. They say it is very much rougher than a football match and possibly it is quite true.

They are just starting the harvest here... the natives hereabouts hate the tanks most cordially. They have good cause to for when a tank wants to go to a certain place it never bothers about roads but simply travels straight there. You can easily picture the result of its journey across this country....

One of our pilots got an M.C. yesterday for general good work. A fellow has to be a pilot to get any decorations and even then his luck has to be in.

Well, I really must stop as I have another letter to write.

Lovingly, Jack.

Since these letters were censored, the families might not have received a complete picture of their experiences. Airmen likely also refrained from sharing some parts of their stories, not wanting to cause their families undue worry.

Once he became operational, Richardson did not write home as much. As he told his mother, "now that I am working I don't have as much time. Three hours a day in the air or even 1 1/2 hours which is a minimum takes the life out of a fellow—makes you dead tired and sleepy and one lacks ambition. So I sometimes don't have enough gumption to write."

In Belgium, Richardson and other airmen from his squadron went swimming. "We take a tender and organize a swimming party to go to the new 'swimming hole' near Clairmarais Forest along a roadway with beautiful trees. It's nice to ride around. The water was fine and we acted like a bunch of small boys." At their drome they sometimes watched movies in the hangars.

Airmen also toured the front, including visiting earlier battlefields. In May 1918, on one of their "dud" days, Richardson and four other fliers from his squadron used a unit tender to see Canadian positions behind the lines. First they drove to Canadian headquarters. "We didn't find many Canucks we knew but we saw the fighting men." Then they drove to Vimy, "where they did such good work. Had tea in a dugout. Saw a little graveyard with nearly 2,000 graves. Saw Chateau Mont St. Eloi shelled by the Huns in 1870 and again in 1917."

Some airmen formed relationships with local women while overseas, especially in Britain, and several New Brunswickers married and returned home with their war brides. They included James Vans McDonald from Campbellton, who served in northern Russia in 1919. Before departing, McDonald married Miss Elsie Mabel Gittins of Manchester, England, on November 4, 1918. By then, Elsie had served throughout the war as a British Red Cross VAD (Voluntary Aid Detachment) nurse. She first joined in November 1914 and worked at the Linden Lea Auxiliary Military Hospital at Brooklands, Cheshire, until 1915. From there she went to No. 5 Hospital in Rouen, France, in 1916, and then No. 4 Northern Hospital in Lincoln, England, from March 1917 to June 1919. Elsie accumulated 6,336 hours of service and received a Red Stripe for efficiency. When McDonald was repatriated to New Brunswick on November 27, 1919, aboard the liner *Royal George*, Elsie accompanied him, and on December 9 they landed in Halifax and made their way home.

Harold Price also married an Englishwoman, Jean Anderson McKay Walker of Clapham, London, on November 5, 1918, while he was recovering from his concussion. Price returned to New Brunswick in December, and Jean joined him in Moncton in early January 1919, a few days before his father died of influenza.

Coping with Stress

Despite all their spare time, the airmen experienced much stress, which they tried to alleviate behind the lines. The air services' high rate of losses took its toll. Weldon Carter wrote about the effects of losses among comrades—"the vacant seats in the mess. However, there is always a chance that the owners of those seats are alive and prisoners of war. This thought affords us some comfort, but sometimes mess is a pretty glum affair. One becomes very strongly attached to the men who fight alongside one every day."

Richardson learned to accept the deaths of comrades. In late May and early June 1918, he missed flying time due to problems with his plane. During his absence, his flight commander, Captain W.J. Cairns, was killed, which hit him hard. "I'm glad I wasn't on that show. I like him so much. I wouldn't care to see him get it. He was a peach of a man. Hell." In early July, another comrade, Mick Mannock, was promoted to major and transferred to command No. 85 Squadron. On July 27, Richardson learned that he had "gone west in a blaze of glory.... I am sure that many of us in #74 can thank our existence to Mick, at some time or other. He always looked after the pilots to keep them out of, or get them out of trouble. What a bloody shame he had to go." Richardson wrote a poem in his memory.

No. 74 Squadron's Captain Edward "Mick" Mannock, VC.
IWM Q60800

"Mick"

There's a lonely cross near Armentieres,
Yet no one knows just where,
It's a spirits cross in memory
Of a leader in the air.
No pompous funeral was his lot,
Nor wrapped in a flag or shroud,

He just "went west" to his place of rest
From the fight amid the cloud.
Yet he was mourned more deeply
By comrades whose feelings were hid,
Men who loved him and served him,
Who knew of the good—he did.
The whitest and squarest and fairest,
Most noted of men who have flown,
Honoured and loved for his bravery,
Yet he went to his grave all alone.
Still in the memory of others,
The memory of Manncok will live,
Knowing he gave most freely
A life that was worthy to give.

—*Len Richardson 1918*

Not all airmen could withstand the stress of combat operations. In mid-June 1918, one of the new pilots in Richardson's squadron was sent home when he refused to fly behind enemy lines. "[He] lost his wings. The C.O. asked him to remove them from his tunic and return to England. [He] has been leaving formation and flying our side of the lines. Probably wasn't entirely his fault, the poor bugger can't even fly. They are sent out here now, totally untrained. Just the same, I think most of us would rather take the hot way out than have the gang think we were yellow."

Some airmen became sick during their service—especially in 1918, when the influenza pandemic began—and had to convalesce. On June 24, Richardson came down with the flu and became quite ill. He stayed in bed all day and could not eat for about five days. By the twenty-eighth, he was able to walk and eat, but the illness spread throughout the squadron—by the thirtieth, only six of the eighteen pilots were "serviceable." To convalesce, Richardson went on a trip to Boulogne and Wimereux, where he spent time on the beach. His temperature remained too high to fly until July 5. By then, only twelve aircraft were operational. After recovering, Richardson got dizzy at higher altitudes or during steep dives for a time. On July 11, he passed out for a few seconds. "Came to in a spin but was still above 10,000 feet so O.K."

Behind the lines, some airmen found solace in religious beliefs and attended church when they could. Richardson was a devout Baptist. In Britain he went to services, even when it was not Baptist. Toward the end of May 1918, he attended his first squadron service since arriving in France, which seemed to have great meaning for him. In a letter to his mother dated May 26, he wrote:

> Our Padre is fine and the service was held in a hangar on benches, boxes, etc. We had a piano to sing to and although we didn't have the pomp, splendour, etc. of a real church, it was one of the best services I ever attended. The Padre (who has been wounded), knew just what he was praying for when he prayed for the soldiers and the wounded. He preached for a little in John 3. Oh! It was good to attend a church service even though it was C. of E. [Church of England]
>
> All of these men who went didn't know if they would see another service or not. Let me tell you, when you don't get a chance to "dress up" and go to church every Sunday and then go and have a service in any old building, some men all greasy, muddy, dressed any old how, you realize just what religion means to some people. I never knew before. Out here we don't know creeds or anything else. It's just having God to fall back on and to know whether we win our scrap or go under that it's just what He wanted. We can't remember that all the time; it seems there are times when we forget it. But we always know.

Richardson endeavoured to draw on his religious beliefs for strength. While he went to church often during training in England, once he reached France things changed and this became more challenging. In a letter to his mother on April 21, 1918, he explained:

Mum, it isn't easy for a fellow to stick to religious principles here because we don't have church and all the other religious environment to help us and after a day of nerve wracking over the lines one seeks light amusement for relaxation and of course I join in. Here a fellow has nothing but his own thoughts to help him and I often wonder if I am right or wrong, but I pray for strength. When I know what is expected of me, as a Christian, I can't help but think I fall down on the job, because as you know, up to a certain point I am full of fun, life and deviltry.

Some airmen also found meaning in nature. Perhaps looking for other sources of inner strength, Richardson became more appreciative of his surroundings once he began combat operations in May 1918. As he wrote to his mother:

The weather is quite fine now and the countryside is getting to be beautiful, fruit trees in bloom, trees all have leaves and crops are progressing. I don't believe I ever noticed the beauties of nature as I do now. It just fills me with awe to see such beautiful country. It's just as pretty as home, only I never realized that home was beautiful. It's a darn shame that such countryside has to be ravaged by war. Near the trenches, between ours and the Hun it is ghastly; whole towns in ruins and nothing but shell holes.

Other airmen were superstitious. Albert Desbrisay Carter kept a shell fragment that was removed from his thigh in 1915 as a souvenir. Lieutenant John Warren Price carried in the inner pocket of his uniform a square silver case, smaller than a cigarette case and flat. Something like a locket, it contained the pictures of his mother and sister. According to a report in the *Moncton Daily Times*, "[t]hey had been with him all through those perilous night raids into Germany, his mascot. 'We fellows are all superstitious.... We carry queer things over with us. Everyone has a mascot, and not much else. We carry a tooth brush, a cheque-book, and some of the fellows carry an extra pair of sox—I don't.'"

Leave and the more extended furloughs gave the airmen a break from active operations. In mid-July 1918, Richardson wrote: "I hope I get leave soon as my nerves are getting edgy." Sometimes airmen from the same hometown stayed in touch once they reached England by taking leave together. Before going to France, Jack Hanson and Hubert Osborne, both observers from Fredericton with No. 55 Squadron, went to London on a pass. They had their photos taken in miniature and placed in lockets that they sent to their mothers. Within a few months both had been killed at the front.

Airmen occasionally returned home from overseas on furlough. In November 1917, after being in Britain and then France for more than a year, Flight Lieutenant Lloyd Sands travelled to Moncton during his twenty-eight-day stay in Canada, surprising his parents by arriving earlier than expected. During his visit, Sands and another airman, Lloyd Murray, were honoured at a banquet held by the Wesley Memorial Church, where both men were members of the choir. Sands returned to Britain in mid-January 1918 and was killed in action on March 22.

Airmen also came home on sick leave to convalesce for extended periods. Lieutenant Robert Shives travelled to New Brunswick in mid-July 1916 after being wounded in late April. According to a report in the

Moncton Daily Times published soon after his arrival, "Lieut. Shives has about recovered from his wounds, although he is obliged to walk with a slight limp." He spent five weeks with his family in Campbellton and also visited Saint John and Fredericton, where he had been a university student. On August 26, he returned to England, where he resumed his duties and was killed in an accident.

Captain Hubert Osborne (Daily Gleaner)

Similarly, Flying Officer Burdette Harmon received a three-month furlough to return home in December 1917 after being wounded in the face. When he arrived in Woodstock, he was met at the train station by the mayor and several other town officials. On February 9, 1918, he married his former UNB classmate Harriet (Hattie) Alleyne Hanselpacker, who was living in Fredericton, and they honeymooned in New York. By the time Harmon returned to the front, Hattie was pregnant and delivered their daughter, Burdetta Wilkins, on November 7, 1918, a few days before the Armistice. By then, Harmon had been dead for almost six months.

Effect on the Home Front

Through their correspondence, furloughs, and other forms of contact, the lives of these airmen profoundly affected family, friends, and community back home, especially when they became casualties. Families and friends were informed when their loved ones were wounded through various sources. In the case of the parents of Flight Lieutenant Louis Ritchie of Saint John, they received a cablegram on March 4, 1918, telling them that their son had been wounded. A few days later, they got a dispatch from Miss Isabel Flinn, a nursing sister formerly from Saint John who was serving in Britain, stating that their son's wounds were not serious.

Perhaps the most difficult time for relatives and friends was when their loved one went missing. For some families, the outcome was favourable when they heard that the airman had eventually turned up in hospital, as was the case for Lieutenant George Winslow Taylor of Saint John. Taylor had been missing since March 13, 1918, and then, according to the *Saint John Globe*, on March 22 his mother learned from Ottawa that, on the fifteenth, he had been admitted to the 5th British Red Cross Hospital in Wimereux suffering from contusions and wounds.

In other cases, the airman had been captured and was in a German POW camp, but his fate was often slow to reach the family. Mrs. Winnifred Heine of Moncton received a letter dated September 23, 1918, from the Air Ministry in London confirming a telegram that was sent notifying Winnifred that her husband, Roland, was missing. "I am to point out that this does not necessarily mean that he is killed or wounded and to say

Lieutenant Louis Ritchie from Saint John is likely the observer
sitting on the aircraft wheel. Courtesy of Margot and David Russell

that you shall be immediately informed as soon as any definite news is received." A short time later, the British Red Cross and Order of St. John acknowledged receipt of a cable from the Heine family asking for information on Roland: "Our 'searchers' carefully question all the wounded in the hospitals in France and England as to what they know of those missing from their own regiments. We are keeping a strict watch for the name on the lists of prisoners which we receive periodically from Germany, in addition to making enquiries in Copenhagen. We have also handed the name to the Central Prisoners of War Committee." Then, on October 22, a cablegram arrived informing Winnifred that Roland was a prisoner of war in Germany.

Mrs. Edward Golding of Saint John received news on October 30, 1917, that her son, Second Lieutenant Kenneth Golding, had been missing since October 24. As the *Saint John Globe* reported, "The dispatch added

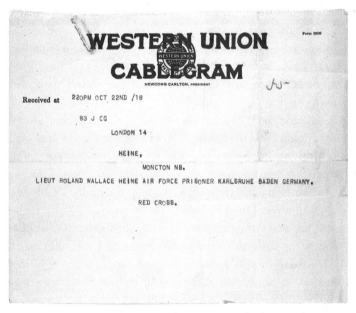

Western Union cablegram informing Winnifred Heine that her husband Roland was a POW. Haney, Heine Family Collection, PANB

that this did not necessarily mean that the young aviator was either killed or wounded. The news, however, will cause much anxiety." During this period of uncertainty, members of the congregation of Saint John's Stone Church mourned his loss and, as the *St. John Standard* reported, his name was added to their honour roll.

Then, in late November, the family finally received welcome news in the form of a report from German newspapers that Golding had been wounded and was a prisoner in Germany. On November 29, W.E. Golding, his brother, got a cable message confirming the news and stating that an effort was being made to locate the hospital where Kenneth was being treated. Over the next weeks, other cables arrived with additional information received from postal cards sent by Golding to a family contact in London. One stated that "he was doing well, was being well treated, and had plenty to eat." As the *Saint John Globe* commented, "This, at least, is gratifying."

Alfred Belliveau's family received official notification that he had gone missing from the government in Ottawa, and a short time later a letter came from a fellow officer, who was unable to tell them what had happened, only that "he was last seen on the other side of the lines among the other machines of the same patrol, but there were clouds about, also they had a pretty tight scrap soon after that....Anyway frankly there is nothing to indicate in the least what his fate is." In early October, after several weeks of anxious waiting for news, they learned that he had been shot down behind enemy lines and become one of the province's several POWs.

For many others, the news was tragic. Families received notice of the death of their loved one from official sources, usually a cable from the Secretary of the War Office in London for airmen serving overseas. They also got letters and sympathy notes from the comrades of their loved one. According to the *Carleton Sentinel*, a few weeks after his son Franklin died, Dr. W.D. Rankin from Woodstock received a letter from the officer commanding No. 18 Squadron, Major C. Carmichael, describing the events of Franklin's loss and offering his condolences.

[Franklin] was one of the pluckiest fellows I have ever had in my squadron and I am sure met the death he would have chosen. He was doing escort to a photographic screen well over the German lines. First they attacked three hostile aircraft and drove them off. They then attacked three more, sending one down in flames, and a second glided down emitting smoke, evidently having been hit in the engine. [Franklin] was standing up firing [over] the top plane at the third machine when a bullet hit him in the head. It was a grand fight against long odds, and it was a splendid death.

I am awfully sorry to lose him. He had done a long spell of good work; took part on many scraps. Only two days before he was in a big melee and shared honors over a machine that fell in our lines. He was always out for a fight. My only apprehension was that he might over step the mark. His pilot, a fellow called Barnard, said he took an awful lot of stopping. Don't think I would try to comfort you with his courage, I am only too glad to be able to say that I was proud to have him in my squadron, and we all admire him as fearless.

He is a great loss. Please accept the deep sympathy of the whole squadron.

Soon afterwards, Dr. Rankin wrote to the squadron asking about Franklin's possessions, especially his diary, and the location of his grave. In a letter dated December 19, held in the New Brunswick Museum Collections, Major Carmichael replied that there was no trace of the diary nor could the grave be found. "I am afraid all graves are soon lost sight of owing to the heavy shelling, but the place where the machine came down is the guide and I like to think of the battered machine as his tombstone. I am more than sorry that it was impossible to bring the body back to the aerodrome, but the difficulties would make it impossible."

Others often had to wait for months before learning the fate of their relative. Lieutenant Morden Mowat was reported missing from No. 11

Squadron on May 16, 1916. By then, the family in Campbellton had already felt the sting of receiving grave news from overseas. Two of Morden's brothers, Godfrey and Oliver, were also at the front, and Godfrey had been wounded in April. A short time later, the Mowats received a letter from a major in Morden's squadron that was printed in the *Cambellton Graphic.*

> I am extremely sorry I have no news to give you of your son as yet. But I hope that no news is good news and that we may shortly hear of his safety. I fear he is a prisoner. He went out in his scout on patrol on the 16th at 5 o'clock in the evening, was sighted once by another of my scouts but since has not been heard of.
>
> I am exceptionally sorry to lose him. He had only been in this squadron a very short time, but had proved himself to be a most fearless flyer.

Several weeks later, the family received more details in a letter dated June 19 from G.K. Tyler, a fellow Canadian, likely from his previous squadron, No. 23. Tyler related that Morden

> went across the lines and did not get back. The Germans reported bringing him down. There is good reason to hope that he is all right. The Germans report did not say that he was killed, as it has in a number of other cases.... Mowat was very popular here and we were awfully sorry when he left us, although it was a step ahead for him and a recognition of his ability as a pilot.

As time passed and the family heard nothing more from official sources, they sought out information on their own. As the *Saint John Globe* reported, they contacted Dr. Roy S. McElwee of New York, who wrote on their behalf to the American consul general in Berlin (at that point, the United States was still a neutral). On October 2, he received a message stating: "I regret to have to inform you that Lieutenant M.M. Mowat...

has not been reported on the lists of prisoners of war in Germany, and I fear the poor man must have been killed without having been identified as the German authorities always report on a man's death if his identification disc is found on his body."

Then, in early December, almost seven months after their son was reported missing, the Mowats received a cablegram from the Secretary of the War Office in London stating: "Deeply regret inform you German government report Second Lieutenant M.M. Mowat died of wounds May 16th. Buried military cemetery Alleud [sic; the cemetery was at Arleux-en-Gohelle]. Army Council express their sympathy." Unfortunately for the Mowat family, in January 1919, Morden's younger brother, Oliver, was also killed, in January 1919 in northern Russia; his body was repatriated for burial in Campbellton.

Other families also went to considerable lengths to discover the fate of their loved one. Lieutenant Talmage Hanning from Fredericton went missing in late November 1916. According to a letter quoted in James Rowinski's *In Perpetuity*, his mother learned more details when his brother, Edward, who was also serving in the RFC, wrote home about what he had discovered.

> I have made many enquiries about Tal all the time from every pilot and observer that I have met. I had at last met an observer who was in No. 9th squadron and also in Tal's flight. (The squadrons are divided into flights). He was a great friend to both Tal and Strauss and the news he has is anything but good. I hesitated to write the news to you. He has no definite news but has made enquiries everywhere after the machine failed to return and finally found a major who was in an observation post, observing for the artillery at the time. This major saw the machine come down, and from the way it fell they gave up hope for them as a wing fell off the machine. One of the officers in the machine was seen to fall out. He was supposed to be the observer as he would not be strapped in. There is no doubt of the observer's fate and has been reported officially killed. It looks

very much as if there was not a chance in the world for Tal. I did not want to write this, but when your letter arrived saying to let you know at once even if I got bad news, I decided to write all I have found out. Tal went out on military observation that morning and after having a few hours over the German lines, he returned to the aerodrome, reporting that it was impossible to see the target owing to the low clouds. Although it was a rotten day, and everybody realized that it was an impossible day, he was sent out again in the afternoon. Tal apparently decided to do the work at all costs and came down to a low altitude, about 1000 feet, and the machine was brought down by a machine gun fire from the ground. It fell close to the German front line trenches. The wreckage of the machine was found when the British advanced, but the ground was so torn up with shell fire that no information could be got from it. I have had strong hopes for Tal, mainly owing to your dreams of him being alive, but the news does not look at all good.

The letter continued:

If Tal is gone mother, you have the satisfaction of knowing that he has been able to kill several hundred Huns besides getting valuable information. There is of course the slimmest chance that he may have landed without being killed, but it is really a very slight one. I am trying to get the name and address of the Major who saw it and expect to be able to, although this observer has forgotten it. I will then write him and get his story in full. I certainly don't like to write this letter, but I believe it would be your wish that I do so. But you must look on it from the brighter side, whether Tal is alive or dead he has done much more than most people do in a lifetime and he had done it well.

Based on the details of his brother's letter and RFC reports, it was determined that Lieutenant Hanning was killed by machine-gun fire at

2:40 p.m., on November 27, 1916, while carrying out a reconnaissance mission at a very low altitude behind German lines near Bapaume, France. His name is found on the Arras Flying Services Memorial.

Similarly, the McNallys of Aberdeen Street in Fredericton were notified that their son, Percy, was missing in mid-August 1917. Then, after the Germans dropped a message into British lines by airplane stating that he had been killed, they received official word in mid-October notifying them of his death. As the *Daily Telegraph* commented, "the hope of his parents that he was a prisoner is now gone."

In those cases when the missing family member became a POW, the family was able to ameliorate the ordeal. At the request of Winnifred Heine, Roland began receiving regular food parcels every five days from the RAF Aid Committee and RAF Prisoners Fund based in London, as well as regular supplies of bread from Switzerland. The family also sent more personal items, including articles of clothing, a Bible, diary, pilot's logbook, leather case containing photographs, and a wallet.

The air war was highly visible and retained some of the nobility lacking in the ground war. Airmen on both sides accounted for and typically honoured the men they shot down. This helped many anxious families discover the fate of their missing sons and brothers, and perhaps find some solace in their grieving.

Chapter Eight

Coming Home and Moving On

Late in the war and following the Armistice, New Brunswick's airmen returned home, some to convalesce, most to resume their peacetime lives. Many found ways to keep their wartime memories alive. The families and communities of fallen airmen also remembered their services through commemoration. As these veterans moved forward with their lives, a few remained connected to their wartime flying experiences either by joining the newly formed Royal Canadian Air Force (RCAF) or pursuing commercial air developments.

Returning Home

Among the first airmen to return to New Brunswick during the war were the wounded, many of whom were still convalescing. After being wounded in February 1918, Flight Lieutenant Louis Ritchie arrived in Saint John via train from Montreal on August 22. He was met at the station by his relatives and a large circle of friends, who accompanied him to his family's summer home in Millidgeville in automobiles decorated with patriotic bunting. The *Saint John Globe* reported that a reception was held that evening at the Royal Kennebecasis Yacht Club. When Ritchie arrived by canoe, he was greeted with cheers and a welcome-home address followed by the City Coronet Band playing "Home Again From A Foreign Shore." Guests danced and drank light refreshments.

The war often cast a shadow over these homecomings. As the *Daily Telegraph* pointed out, as "joyful as it might seem, however, it was not without its tinge of sorrow as among the welcoming party were near relatives of Mrs. Clair Gilmour, whose husband was a near friend and chum of Lieutenant Ritchie and who was shot down by the enemy and died some time ago."

These welcome-home gatherings continued for some time. On February 1, 1919, the parents of Cadet Pierce John Brewster hosted a party for their son in their home in Hampton. Brewster had enlisted in the 6th Canadian Mounted Rifles and went overseas with the regiment to France in October 1915. He was wounded in September 1916, and after recovering joined the Fort Garry Horse, with which he served until February 1918. He then joined the RFC, but did not complete his pilot training before the war ended. According to an article in the *Daily Telegraph*, "the house was neatly decorated for the occasion with flags. The evening was pleasantly spent with games, music and dancing.... Cheers were given for the returned heroes, of which there were a number present, and the singing of the national anthem brought the evening to a close."

Some wounded airmen came home on hospital ships. In June 1919, Flight Lieutenant George Wootten arrived in Portland, Maine, aboard His Majesty's Hospital Ship *Essequibo*. His parents travelled from Andover to accompany him back to New Brunswick, where he entered the military hospital in Fredericton. Later, he spent several weeks with his family before returning to the hospital.

Other airmen who returned home after the Armistice needed time to convalesce. On November 7, 1918, Lieutenant Kenneth Golding underwent a medical board review that assessed him as being medically unfit for duty, and he received leave to Canada. In early December 1918, he arrived at New York on the SS *Lapland* and returned to New Brunswick by train, reaching Saint John on the seventh. A report in the *St. John Standard* a few days later suggests Golding was still recovering from his ordeal: "The returned officer is as reticent as a Yale lock regarding his experiences while in action or while a prisoner, and tells his relatives and friends that he is forgetting everything, or trying to do so. He is fast regaining his lost health and will in the near future be himself again." Among Golding's earliest activities on his road to recovery was to visit Mr. and Mrs. F.B. Edgecombe in Fredericton, whose airman son, Charles, had died in a flying accident in early October 1918, and to attend religious services at Saint John's Stone Church, where his death had been mistakenly commemorated more than a year earlier.

When Captain Alvah Good arrived home on the *Essequibo* in early April 1919, he was still suffering from the effects of his fractured skull, and was admitted to the military hospital in Fredericton between April 12 and April 28 for further treatment; he returned periodically for the next several months. According to his CEF service file, he mainly complained of insomnia, poor concentration, difficult coordination, and an unreliable memory. As treatment he received daily general massages followed by rest. By October, when he was discharged, he felt much better, although he still had trouble sleeping. He died on October 27, 1962.

After the war, several New Brunswickers served with the Canadian air service in Britain. Upon being repatriated to Britain from German POW camps, Major Albert D. Carter was hospitalized at the beginning of January 1919 suffering from influenza. After recovering, he joined No. 123 Squadron, (Canadians), RAF, part of the Canadian Air Force in England, on January 24, 1919. He became a flight commander in No. 123 Squadron — the day-bomber squadron — a testament to his skill and record of service during the war. At some point, he led one of the squadrons that escorted the march of the returning overseas troops through London. He was also presented with a captured German Fokker D.VII airplane by the Canadian overseas government.

On May 22, 1919, the twenty-seven-year-old Carter was killed when the Fokker D.VII plane he was flying during a training exercise "collapsed" in mid-air and crashed to the ground. He was buried at Old Shoreham Cemetery in England. Shortly afterwards, a court of inquiry was held at Shoreham to ascertain the circumstances of his death. Several witnesses were called, including an officer from "C" Flight who flew the

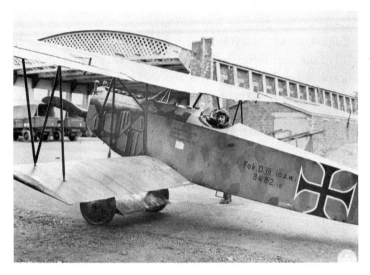

Major Albert Desbrisay Carter sitting in the cockpit of the German D.VII Fokker fighter he was presented with by the Canadian overseas government. 2007.07/1657, Mount Allison University Archives

Fokker the day before without problem, "C" Flight's chief mechanic and fitter sergeant, who verified its soundness, and Captain Carl Falkenberg, commander of "A" Flight, who practised combat with Carter for about thirty minutes, and when returning to the aerodrome saw the wings of the Fokker break away after Carter pulled out of a dive and crashed into the ground. Upon visiting the scene of the accident before the airplane was removed, the inquest found that the "studs fastening planes to struts sheared in all cases. Port rear top strut showed flaw in metal at the break." As the inquest report in Carter's CEF service file shows, they found that the cause of the accident was "that the machine collapsed in coming out of a dive." The officer commanding No. 1 Canadian Wing, RAF, Lieutenant-Colonel Robert Leckie, concurred with the findings, and added: "There were still many ex-German Fokkers and Rumplers at Shoreham, and as peacetime operations left little to do, the Canadians often used them for aerobatics." (Leckie later became an air marshal and Chief of the Air Staff of the RCAF from 1944 to 1947.)

In 2009, Canadian aviation historian Stewart K. Taylor published a two-part article on Carter in the *Cross and Cockade International* journal. In it, he presents a surprising conclusion based on an interview he conducted fifty-six years after Carter's death with the former "A" Flight Commander of No. 1 Squadron, CAF, who claimed that, "although the court of enquiry did not reach a verdict on the cause of this fatality it was later learned, and hushed up, that the bolts connecting the interplane cabane struts with the upper wing had been partially sawn off. Considering the attitude of the ground crew at the time it was impossible to bring the culprit, or culprits to trial and the actual participants were never identified." As shown above, however, the damage to the Fokker's wing was known to the inquiry at the time, reported in its proceedings, and a cause for the accident assigned based on its investigation.

Carter's death was widely reported throughout the province. According to a *Daily Telegraph* report published in May 1919, "His fine record in the Air Force is one of which the province should be very proud as he is probably the finest airman New Brunswick has produced. Major Carter was well known throughout the province and very popular, especially with the originals of the 26th." Similarly, the *St. John Standard* wrote:

> The whole province mourns the loss of one who brought credit to his native heath, both as a fighter in the infantry ranks and after in the air. In the air he was one of the leading Canadian aces, having to his credit no less that thirty-two [*sic*; the actual number was twenty-eight] enemy planes, and was regarded by his companions as one of the most daring fighters and scouts in the R.F.C.... The officers of his own squadron were loud in his praise and gave him the reputation of being absolutely fearless and tireless.... He was a dead shot and this fact accounted for some of his success in dealing with Fritz.

Carter's comrade and friend from the 140th Battalion, Captain Stuart Bell, commented on the irony of his death. He had visited Carter at Shoreham three weeks before his crash, spending five days as his guest.

"While there I had the pleasure of going up several times with him and it seems the irony of fate that he should after battling successfully with the Hun and making the record he did, come to his death at the drome where he took his first flight into the air."

After being a POW in Germany Lieutenant Lee Roy Brown was repatriated to Britain, where, on March 28, 1919, he too joined No. 123 Squadron a few months after Carter. As Valerie Evans shows in *We That Are Left*, on February 5, 1920, Brown transferred to the RAF's No. 24 Squadron, and in 1924 he joined the RAF reserve as a wing commander. He returned to active duty during the Second World War. Afterwards, Brown returned to Canada and lived in British Columbia until he died in 1979.

Remembrance

Both the returned airmen and their families and communities found ways to remember their wartime service. While some veterans preferred to remain silent about their experiences, others were anxious to tell their stories and enlighten the public about air warfare. Several made public presentations. In early February 1919, Lieutenant Roland Heine gave a talk to the Canadian Club at the Aberdeen Hall in Moncton about his life as a prisoner of war. It was based largely on his letters that had appeared in local newspapers several months earlier as well as new information. According to the *Moncton Daily Times*, the large audience "thoroughly enjoyed the lecture from start to finish, frequently breaking into applause." At the end of his presentation "Heine called for three cheers for the Empire and its defenders, and also thanked the audience for their vote of thanks."

On February 13, 1919, pilot Frank Nicholson presented a lantern show depicting "AirCraft in the Great War," illustrated by fifty slides at the vestry of the McColl Methodist Church in St. Stephen. As an article in the *St. Croix Courier* stated, "this is a rare opportunity to hear one of our returned men speak of the work that he knows so well through his experience as an airman at the front." After the address, the *Courier* reported that Nicholson's talk "was intensely interesting, both in his address when introducing his subject and also in the explanations of the various aeroplanes thrown up on the canvas. At the close of the address a unanimous vote of thanks was tendered to the Captain, coupled with the acknowledgements of its educational value."

During and after the war, some airmen joined veterans' organizations that actively kept alive the memory of their fallen comrades. Among the charter members of the Byng Boys Club formed in 1921 in Saint John were Louis Ritchie and Edward Cronin, who were present for the visit of the governor general, Viscount Byng, to New Brunswick on July 10, 1923. Later, Cronin moved to the United States; he died tragically on April 3, 1950, when he fell in front of a subway train in Brooklyn. According to the *St. Croix Courier*, "he was 60 years of age and had weak turns at different times recently. It is believed that he suffered one of these attacks in the subway which resulted in his death."

Viscount Byng of Vimy visiting the Byng Boys Club House, Pleasant Point, Milford, NB, July 10, 1923. Louis Ritchie is present in the third row on the far right, and Edward Cronin stands in the centre row fifth from the right, beside Byng. NBM Albert Alfred Dodge fonds/Dodge, AA-1

The "fallen," those who died during the war, were remembered at home both during the war and afterwards. New Brunswick's local communities grieved the loss of their hometown airmen and commemorated them publicly. Memorial services were often held in the fallen airman's hometown shortly after the family received word of its loss. In early November 1916, a service was conducted at St. Paul's Church in Woodstock following the news of Franklin Rankin's death. According to an article in the *Carleton Sentinel*, the church "was crowded to the doors and many were not able to get in." During the service, Reverend Frank Baird captured the mood often expressed during these times, stating: "So far as I have been able to ascertain [Rankin] was not only the first of the town to enlist, but was the first also to make the supreme sacrifice. Inspired by a soldier's spirit, he took a soldier's risk, met a soldiers' death and sleeps in a soldier's grave."

Local funerals were held for those airmen who died outside the province after their bodies were repatriated to their hometown for burial. At least two died from illnesses. Cadet Arthur Vernon Hatch of Saint John died of pneumonia in May 1918 in Toronto while undergoing training.

(from left) Graves of Lieutenant John W. Price and Cadet A. Vernon Hatch.
Author's photos

His body was brought home for burial in Fernhill Cemetery in Saint John. Similarly, Lieutenant John Warren Price from Moncton died in the military hospital in Hamilton, Ontario, on October 9, 1918. His body was carried to Moncton on the Maritime Express train, accompanied by his father. A private service was held at the family residence; afterwards the funeral cortege proceeded to Elmwood Cemetery in Moncton for the internment. It was headed by the Citizens' Band and members of the Masonic Order, of which Price was a member, and the Great War Veterans' Association (GWVA), a forerunner of the Royal Canadian Legion, who preceded the hearse to the grave. The casket was draped in the Union Jack and a Masonic service was conducted. According to the *Moncton Daily Times*, "there were many handsome floral tributes expressive of sincere sympathy for the bereaved and evidencing the high esteem in which the deceased young officer was held."

At least four other airmen died in airplane accidents during training in Canada or the United States and were sent home for burial. Cadet Evan McMillan from Durham Centre in Restigouche County was killed on January 21, 1918, in a mid-air collision with another cadet's aircraft at the Armour Heights Camp at Toronto. He was buried at the New Mills Protestant Cemetery near Jacquet River. As noted earlier, Cadet Edgar LeBlanc from Moncton died on April 29, 1918, in an airplane accident at the Mohawk Aviation Camp at Deseronto, Ontario. His body was brought back to Moncton on May 2, and he was buried in the Shediac Road Roman Catholic Cemetery, with members of the GWVA in attendance.

Similarly, Cadets Joseph Brosnan of Saint John and Gordon Mott of Campbellton died at a training facility in Fort Worth, Texas, during the winter of 1917/18. Both of their bodies were brought home for burial at Saint Joseph's Cemetery in Saint John and Campbellton Rural Cemetery, respectively. The body of Cadet Brosnan returned by train from Texas to Saint John via Boston after a journey of five days. He was buried on February 19, 1918. A report in the *Daily Telegraph* captured the spirit of the event as the funeral procession made its way from St. Peter's Church to the cemetery.

The body was then placed in the hearse and covered with a Union Jack and the funeral cortege swung into line and proceeded to the new Catholic cemetery.... Following a number of coaches, came a barouche laden with magnificent floral tributes, a firing squad of forty soldiers from the depot battalion, the depot battalion band, the hearse, surrounded by six pall-bearers from the Knights of Columbus, mourners, officers of the depot battalion and others who have returned from the battle fields of France, [and] members of the War Veterans Association.... As the procession wended its way along Main Street, hundreds of people lined the sidewalks.

Finally, at least three other airmen who died overseas in Britain in accidents were repatriated by their families for burial. The first was Robert Shives, who was killed by an accidental machine-gun discharge. His remains were brought home aboard the steamship *Ionian*, arriving in Saint John at the beginning of January 1917. His oak casket was removed to the chapel at Fernhill Cemetery, where his burial took place on January 2 next to his father's grave. Several members of the family, including his mother, were present, as well as many members of the military.

Lieutenant Jarvis McLellan was also buried in Fernhill Cemetery in Saint John in August 1918. After his accidental death in July, McLellan's parents chose to have his body repatriated; it arrived in Saint John by ship on August 14. The next afternoon, his remains were moved from the family residence to Centenary Church, where a funeral service took place with full military honours. As the *Daily Telegraph* reported, "The church was crowded with citizens from every walk of life including the city fathers, representatives of the military and naval departments and a large assemblage of citizens and friends of the family." The casket was draped with the Union Jack. Reverend H.A. Goodwin delivered an eloquent eulogy in which he "spoke feelingly of the young officer who so heroically and bravely in the prime of life had freely given his services to his country." He also spoke of the sacrifice that was befalling the mothers of such heroes. "They, too, are sharing in a special manner the sacrifices of their

(clockwise from top left) Graves of Captain Robert K. Shives and Lieutenant Jarvis O. McLellan, Fernhill Cemetery, Saint John, and Lieutenant Earle Scovil, St. Stephen Rural Cemetery.
Author's photos

boys." Afterwards, a large funeral procession led by the New Brunswick Depot Battalion and a firing party from the No. 7 Canadian Garrison Regiment proceeded to Fernhill Cemetery, where McLellan was buried in the family plot. Six officers from the Garrison Regiment bore the bier upon which the casket rested. The Last Post was sounded and three volleys fired over the grave.

Lastly, Lieutenant Earle Markee Scovil of St. Stephen was buried on March 2, 1919, in the St. Stephen Rural Cemetery. Born in St. Stephen on April 2, 1897, the eighteen-year-old Scovil enlisted with his parents' consent in a reinforcement draft of the 55th Battalion in April 1915. After arriving overseas, he joined the 1st Battalion in France in September, and was wounded on June 22, 1916. As a sergeant, he was awarded the Military Medal for bravery in the field during the Battle of the Somme. In November, he returned to New Brunswick to join the 236th Battalion as a lieutenant and then, after returning to Britain, joined the RFC in early March 1918. On July 21, 1918, he was killed accidentally at Netheravon, in Wiltshire, when "his machine stalled while flying at an insufficient height to resume control." He was buried in a nearby church cemetery. In February 1919, his body was exhumed, transferred to Saint John on the steamer *Scotian*, and then sent to St. Stephen for interment under the auspices of the GWVA. As the *Daily Telegraph* wrote, the funeral procession was "said to have been a mile long."

Families also remembered their loved ones who died and were buried overseas in local cemeteries with memorials engraved on family headstones and footstones. Burdette Harmon was killed in action in France on May 10, 1918, and buried in the Villers-Bretonneux Military Cemetery. He is commemorated in two places in the Woodstock Methodist Cemetery: on a footstone marker, along with his parents, Louisa and Allison — father survived son by twenty-two years — and on the gravestone of his widow, Hattie, who died in 1957. Their daughter, Burdetta (named after her father), is buried alongside her mother. John Gibson is remembered on the headstone of his father, Alexander, in the Marysville United Church Cemetery. Albert Carter's name appears on the headstone of his parents in the Point de Bute Cemetery. And a memorial to Morden Mowat is found on the Mowat family headstone in the Campbellton Rural Cemetery. These family memorials, found in cemeteries all across the province, show the far-reaching effects of the war.

The province's fallen airmen were also remembered in many other ways. After the war, their medals were sometimes presented to family in private ceremonies. For example, in January 1919, Hattie Harmon, Burdette's widow, received his Military Cross from the private secretary of New Brunswick's lieutenant governor in Woodstock. Many newspapers printed obituaries that extolled their patriotic virtues. Writing

Family memorials for Lieutenant Morden Mowat and Major Albert D. Carter.
Author's photos

about Harmon, the *Carleton Sentinel* pronounced that "his young life was sacrificed for a noble cause. His memory will always be honored and revered —a priceless heritage to those to whom he was most dear. Boys like Burdette Harmon will save our institutions, and save our honor unsullied as an inspiration and example for the boys and girls who will only know of this titanic conflict through the pages of history."

In April 1919, the parents of Jarvis McLellan received some comfort in their grieving when they obtained "in a very curious way" the Henry Wadsworth Longfellow book Jarvis had received in school as a birthday present and taken overseas with him. When a Montreal newspaper revealed how the book that bore Jarvis's name on the fly leaf had been found, the McLellans contacted the current owner in Philadelphia, "who said it had been handed to him by a dying [American] soldier at the last battle of Ypres with the request it be sent to the mother of the original owner." According to the *Daily Telegraph*, the McLellans "rejoiced to have this memento of their lost son returned to them." As the article concluded, "the strangest part of the returning of the book is that Lieutenant McLellan was on aerial patrol duty on the North Sea and on the Tyne and how it came in the possession of a soldier in Ypres can only be conjectured."

The names of fallen airmen are also inscribed on the numerous community war memorials and cenotaphs located throughout the province.

(above) Stained glass window for Lieutenant Franklin Rankin in Memorial Hall, University of New Brunswick. Author's photo

(below) The names of the fallen on the plaque in Memorial Hall, University of New Brunswick. Lori Quick (Courtesy UNB Art Centre)

Among the 106 names appearing on the Fredericton War Memorial are airmen Charles Edgecombe, Talmage Hanning, Hubert Osborne, Jack Hanson, and Purves Loggie. The Carleton County Cenotaph features the names of Burdette Harmon and Franklin Rankin. John Gibson's name is on the Marysville Cenotaph. The name of Albert Carter appears on the cenotaph in Port Elgin. Earle Scovil's name is on the St. Stephen Cenotaph.

Lastly, the names of the fallen airmen are found on numerous school, church, and other community honour rolls, plaques, and memorial windows. The University of New Brunswick's memorial plaque in Memorial Hall lists John Gibson, Burdette Harmon, Talmage Hanning, John Hanson, Hubert Osborne, Purves Loggie, and Robert K. Shives. A memorial window for Franklin Rankin is also found in Memorial Hall. The student memorial for the Wesleyan Academy names Charles Edgecombe and Hubert Osborne, while Mount Allison University's lists Albert D. Carter, Charles H. Edgecombe, Donald G. Mott, and D. Evan McMillan. The names of Arthur Hatch and Franklin Rankin appear on the honour roll of the Rothesay Netherwood School.

Churches also remembered their parishioners. For example, a plaque in St. Paul's Presbyterian Church in Fredericton includes the names of Talmage Hanning and Purves Loggie. The pew, choir stalls, and organ in the Anglican Christ Church in Campbellton are dedicated to the memory of Captain Robert Shives and his father, Kilgour Shives.

Post-war Lives

After the war, several of New Brunswick's veteran airmen joined the RCAF, including Leigh Stevenson, who had a long and distinguished career. In 1921, he returned to the west and briefly worked with the Department of the Interior's Forestry Service in Manitoba as a seaplane pilot until joining the air force and serving throughout the inter-war years. In the 1920s and 1930s, Stevenson held various posts throughout Canada and England, where he was an RCAF liaison officer. He commanded air stations, including Winnipeg's, and helped to establish several new airports. In 1936, he led a large-scale air search in the Northwest Territories.

Air Vice-Marshal Leigh F. Stevenson having tea with King George VI; Stevenson was Air Officer Commanding the RCAF in Britain from October 1940 to November 1941. Courtesy of Harold Wright

During the Second World War, he held several key posts, including Air Officer Commanding (AOC) of the British Commonwealth Air Training Plan's No. 4 Training Command in western Canada, AOC of the RCAF in Great Britain in London, and OC of Western Air Command. After the war, he entered politics, becoming a Member of the Legislative Assembly in British Columbia. He died in Vancouver in March 1989.

After returning home from the war, Royden Foley established an automobile business in Saint John, which he later sold to K.C. Irving, and moved to Hamilton, Ontario. He joined the Royal Canadian Auxiliary Air Force and became second-in-command of Hamilton's No. 119 Squadron. He was also active with civilian flying clubs. In May 1928, an article in the *Brantford Expositor* described how he flew an Avro Avian aircraft distributing pamphlets over Brantford for the Brant-Norfolk Aero Club.

Foley continued to serve with the RCAF during the Second World War. Initially, he was the commanding officer of the RCAF recruiting depot in Windsor, Ontario. Later, he was transferred to Ottawa and then

Vancouver, where he served at the seaplane base at Jericho Beach. Then he took a special course in aerial navigation at Trenton, Ontario, and was sent to Malton when the first elementary flying corps was opened under the British Commonwealth Air Training Plan. By August 1940, he had been promoted to squadron leader and was appointed to No. 3 Training Command. Eventually, he became a wing commander. Foley died on March 18, 1958. His connection to the Wright brothers stayed with him for the rest of his life.

Michael Lawrence Doyle, the DFC recipient from River Louison, also continued his air service after the war. On April 1919, he joined the CAF. Then, during the Second World War, he served with the RCAF, initially as a flight lieutenant administrative officer in November 1940. Later, he moved to No. 3 Training Command headquarters, and in February 1942 was promoted squadron commander. He was released from service on September 5, 1944. He died on February 2, 1953.

Other New Brunswick RAF veterans of the Great War remained active airmen in commercial flying ventures. Shortly after the war, Burpee Hay became manager of the Aviation Company of Canada. In January 1919, he met with the Saint John Board of Trade to discuss a proposal to establish an aviation station in the city. According to an article in the *Saint John Globe*, after Hay had outlined the plan and some discussion had taken place, a committee was appointed to meet with Hay and get full details on the scheme and report back at a later meeting. No other details about the company or Hay's role are known. Hay died on December 6, 1981.

Another provincial airman who became active in post-war commercial aviation was Frederick Harold Turner of Saint John. He and his war bride wife, Sarah, moved after the war, eventually settling in Calgary. In 1929, Harold helped to establish the Rutledge Air Service Limited along with William Rutledge, who was one of Turner's RFC instructors during the war. According to an article in the *Calgary Albertan* in July 1929, Turner was a "specialist in cloud flying commercial pilot of the Calgary Aero Club, expert in aeroplane construction, who will also take charge of commercial flying activities and instruction of students." In 1931, Turner moved on to join the western air mail service. When it was cancelled in March 1932,

Turner set up Airportation Limited to establish aerial operations linking various settlements in far northern Alberta and the Northwest Territories. The Turners moved to Fort McMurray to establish a base for the company, but Harold died suddenly in October 1932.

Many of the airmen who survived the war resumed their pre-war lives. Louis Ritchie completed his law degree and became a successful lawyer, later serving as a member of the New Brunswick Court of Appeal until he retired in 1969. According to his daughter, Margot, in 1926 he married Nellie Gilmour, his childhood neighbour from Millidgeville and widow of his friend and fellow airman, Clair Gilmour; Clair Jr. became his stepson. Unfortunately, Nellie died about a year later from leukemia. Louis died on December 28, 1981, and is buried in St. Joseph's Cemetery in Saint John.

Several young airmen returned to school after completing their service. Lieutenant Alexander McMorran from Oak Hill attended the Khaki University set up by the Canadian Army at Ripon, Yorkshire, in 1919 while waiting to return home. Cecil Langstroth from Hampton was a student at Mount Allison University when he joined up in August 1916. After returning home from overseas, he resumed his studies. Frederick "Ted" Coster from Saint John was also a student at the time of his enlistment in Toronto on June 10, 1918. After his discharge, he left for Dalhousie College in January 1919. Finally, James Russell Morash from Sussex enlisted as a cadet in Toronto on November 7, 1918, only four days before the Armistice. He was discharged on January 1, 1919, after only fifty days of service and, as the *Kings County Record* wrote, intended to complete his high school diploma during the remainder of the school year.

Some veterans joined the province's business community. Kenneth Irving returned home to Bouctouche and entered the merchant trade, sold automobiles, and ran local gas stations. He moved to Saint John, where he continued to expand his service station business, founding K.C. Irving Gas and Oil Ltd. and selling petrol throughout much of southern New Brunswick, and parts of Nova Scotia and Prince Edward Island. He also expanded the J.D. Irving forest operations founded by his father into the pulp and paper, newsprint, and veneer industries. In time he entered into shipbuilding and shipping, trucking, and many other businesses. During the Second World War, his veneer plant built landing barges that were used on D-Day. By the time he died in 1992, Irving was the head of one of Canada's largest business empires.

Many who re-entered civilian life moved elsewhere and built new lives. After Alfred Belliveau returned home, he ceased to be seconded to the RAF on April 13, 1919, and was discharged shortly afterwards. In 1927, Alfred moved to the United States and in 1936 became an American citizen. Initially, he lived in Chicago, where he worked at Sears Roebuck & Co. and then enrolled in the Coyne Electrical School, taking courses in electrical engineering. Afterwards, he got a job at the Automatic Electric Plant in its development laboratories — in time, his name appeared on seven US patents. During the Depression, however, when the department shut down, he worked at odd jobs until returning later to the company's Patents Department. In 1938, his sister, Alma, joined him in Chicago and became his housekeeper. Belliveau took more correspondence courses and became a director with the company's credit union. The company grew significantly during the Second World War, and he continued studying, eventually earning a BA from De Paul University.

In September 1959, Alfred retired at age sixty-five, and he and Alma moved to Newburyport, Massachusetts, where they lived with Alfred's brother Edward and his wife. In retirement Alfred continued to work with credit unions as well as carrying out technical translations from French to English for patent attorneys until 1971. He died on January 24, 1985, at age ninety.

Although the number of airmen from New Brunswick who served during the Great War was proportionately smaller than those from some other parts of the country, those who enlisted made an important contribution to the air war. They served in all theatres and carried out all the missions the British air services undertook. Those who survived left a hard-won legacy. As Alfred Belliveau wrote, when he returned home, "there of course was a joyful reunion, with the son who had defied the lightning in one of the bitterest wars ever fought and in which some of the combatants for the first time flew through the air to attack one another." Many others, however, paid a heavy price for their efforts. At least twelve airmen were wounded during the war, and twenty-nine died at home or overseas, due to accidents or combat. Today, the toll of their endeavours can be seen first-hand throughout the province in its places of commemoration, cemeteries, museums, and many other sites.

Appendix

New Brunswick Airmen
during the Great War

It is difficult to know how many airmen from New Brunswick served during the Great War. Wise's *Official History* cites 172 enlistments in the province, but many more names appear in this appendix. They include all airmen born in New Brunswick, even if they had since moved away and enlisted elsewhere during the war, as well as some who were born outside the province but grew up locally. In many cases, their parents were New Brunswickers who had moved outside the province for a time but then returned to live. Also, in early 1918, provincial newspapers identified the names of some cadets and mechanics who could not be found in official records. Presumably, they did not pass the medical examination or for some other reason were not accepted. The 252 names appearing in this appendix are only those that could be confirmed through official records. Every effort has been made to make this list as comprehensive as possible, but some names might be missing.

Name	Birthplace/Residence
Addy, Gordon Chelsey Martin	Moncton
Alchorn, Charles Montagu	Saint John
Alward, Owen Doyle	Havelock
Archibald, Wesley Alexander	Flatlands
Armstrong, Joseph Louis	Saint John
Atherton, Alfred Byron	Woodstock
Babbitt, Thomas Emerson	Gibson
Barnaby, Hazen Ottis	Saint John
Barr, Herbert Carrick	Saint John
Bayne, Blair Edmundston	Moncton
Bedell, Vaughan Byron	Andover
Bell, Lawrence McLean	Moncton
Belliveau, Alfred Hilaire	Fredericton

Name	Birthplace/Residence
Bernier, George Mathew	Connors
Beveridge, Chester Gladstone	Arcadia, NS/Fairville
Bishop, Stanley Emerson	Hillsboro
Blair, Gordon Williston	Shediac
Boudreau, Joseph Armond Ernest	Campbellton
Boudreau, Joseph Emery	East Bathurst
Bourgeois, James Philippe	Moncton
Boutin, Wilfrid Raymond	West Arichat, NS/St. Stephen
Boyer, George Arthur	Hartland/Lowell, MA
Brewster, Pierce John	Hampton
Brosnan, Joseph Daniel	Saint John
Brown, John Renwick	Coal Branch
Brown, Lee Roy Lowerison	Westmorland Point
Bull, Alfred Teed	Woodstock
Busby, William Herbert	Milltown
Campbell, Walter Graham	Saint John
Campbell, William Ernest	St. George
Carter, Albert Desbrisay	Point de Bute
Carter, John Wilbert	Salisbury
Carter, William Allison Weldon	Saint John/Fredericton
Cawley, Charles Frederick	St. George
Christie, Harold Leonard	Saint John
Clark, Charles Arthur	Saint John
Clarke, Alan Douglas	Saint John
Clowes, Stanley Gordon Jaffrey	Oromocto
Cochrane, James Nelson	Moncton
Comeau, Fabian Louis	Wayne, MI/Saint John
Copp, Edgar Allison	Sackville
Coram, Robert McIntyre	Saint John
Coster, Frederick Edwin	Saint John
Coveney, Wilfred Martin	England/Fredericton
Creaghan, Gerald	Newcastle
Creaghan, Thomas Cyril	Newcastle
Creaghan, William Vincent	Newcastle
Cripps, Heber John	Sussex
Cronin, Edward John	Milltown/Saint John
Crowley, John Arthur	Fredericton
Cyr, Arthur Joseph	Saint-Hilaire

Name	Birthplace/Residence
Daley, Charles Albert	Jacquet River
Daley, Warnock Bernard	Elgin
Davis, Robert Wesley	Saint John
Dawson, Stephen Arthur	Saint John
Demers, Joseph Cleo	Newcastle
Doiron, Léo	Shediac
Doody, Frank Patrick	Saint John
Douglas, Charles Colpitts	Petitcodiac
Doyle, Michael Lawrence	River Louison
Drake, William Clive	Saint John
Drew, Lloyd Addington	Long Point
Dunn, David Stanley	Gagetown
Eddy, Arthur Wilmot	Chatham
Eden, Elvin Roy	Irish Town
Edgecombe, Charles Hedley	Fredericton
Edington, John Bartleman	Moncton?
Emery, Alban Scovil	Saint John
Ervine, Frederick Ward	Andover
Evans, Henry Clark	Saint John
Evans, John Harper	Moncton
Eveleigh, Edgar Percy	Sussex
Ferris, Harold Bunting	Saint John
FitzGerald, Cecil Desmond	Fredericton
FitzRandolph, Archibald Menzies	Saint John
Fletcher, Harold John	Upham
Fletcher, Wilfred George	Upham
Foley, Gerald	Newcastle
Foley, J. Royden	Saint John
Folkins, Joseph Chipman	Woodstock
Forsyth, Harold Kitchener	Saint John
Fournier, Ludger Louis	Saint-Léonard
Fraser, John Moore	Grand Manan
Fritz, Horatio Warren Douglas	Saint John
Gallant, Frank/Francois Joseph	Rogersville
Gibson, Harry Arthur	Fredericton
Gibson, John Thomas	Marysville
Gilbert, James Simonds	Rothesay
Gillies, Myles Alton	Springfield

Name	Birthplace/Residence
Gillmore, Cecil Foster	Moncton
Gilmour, Arthur Clair	Saint John
Givan, Harry Edward	Shediac
Golding, Kenneth Logan	Saint John
Good, George Alvah	Woodstock/Fredericton
Grant, William Howe	St. Stephen
Graves, Charles Leo	Jacksonville
Haley, Raymond Robins	Saint John
Hall, Frank Henley	Saint John
Hanning, John Edward	Fredericton
Hanning, James Talmage	Fredericton
Hanson, John Clarence	Sussex/Fredericton
Harmon, Burdette William	Peel/Woodstock
Harrington, Edward Fairweather	Hampton
Hatheway, Clarence Murray	Annandale
Hatch, Arthur Vernon	Saint John
Hay, Burpee McLeod	Woodstock
Heine, Roland Wallace	Moncton
Henderson, Harold Allen	Moncton
Hicks, Cecil Gilbert	Petitcodiac
Hicks, Curtis Lemont	Hampton
Hieatt, Harry Ernest	Saint John
Higginson, Ernest George	Saint John
Hurley, Percy Raymond	Saint John
Irons, Reginald Bryant	Moncton
Irvine, Walter Holland	Chicago, IL/St. Mary's
Irving, Charles Ernest	Moncton
Irving, Kenneth Colin	Bouctouche
Irving, William Henry	Moncton
Jack, Robert Lawrence Munro	Chatham
Jardine, Arthur	Nordin
Johnson, Joseph Alonzo	Richibucto
Johnston, Robin Louis	Saint John
Jones, George Willis	Summerside, PEI/Moncton
Jones, John Blair	Saint John
Jordan, John Nathaniel	Saint John
Keeley, Frederick Joseph	Saint John
Kennedy, Arthur James	Rothesay

Name	Birthplace/Residence
Kennedy, Frederick	Shediac
Kent, William Morley	Bathurst
Kirk, James Herbert	Sussex
Kitchen, George Walter	Fredericton
Landry, Wilfred Andrew	Dorchester
Langstroth, Cecil Craven	Hampton
LeBlanc, Aimé	Saint-Anselme
LeBlanc, Edgar Patrick	Moncton
Léger, Aimé Antoine	Cocagne
Lockhart, William Stanley	Moncton
Lounsbury, George Holland	Queensbury
Macarthur, James Wilbur	Newcastle/Québec,QC
MacDonald, Donald Angus	Saint John
MacLatchy, James Penn Cauldwell	Moncton
McDonald, James Vans	Campbellton/Vernon, BC
McElveney, Robert Lee	Fredericton
McFarlane, Kenneth	Nashwaaksis
McGrath, Henry D'Arcy	Dorchester
McInerney, Ralph	Richibucto
McKenzie, Kenneth	Dalhousie
McKinnon, Archibald Clifford	Sussex
McLellan, Jarvis Oldfield	Saint John
McLeod, George Egerton Stuart	Saint John
McManamin, Stephen Basil	Fredericton
McManus, James Wilfred	West Bathurst
McMillan, Donald Evan	Durham Centre
McMillan, James Gordon	Durham Centre
McMillan, Robert Earnshaw	Durham Centre
McMorran, Alexander Morrison	Oak Hill
McNally, Percy Byron	Fredericton/Calgary, AB
McNaughton, William	Black River/Chatham
McNutt, George Raymond	Newcastle/Fredericton
McWha, Frederick William	St. Stephen
Malcolm, Charles Gordon	Saint John
Malcolm, Jack E.	Campbellton
Mann, George Isaac	Chatham
Manning, Lawrence Edward	Saint John
Meahan, Bernard	West Bathurst

Name	Birthplace/Residence
Melanson, Albert Joseph	South Bathurst
Miller, Emery Earl	Cumberland Bay
Mitchell, Thomas	Saint John
Morash, James Russell	Sussex
Mott, David Gordon	Dalhousie
Mowat, Godfrey Alden	Campbellton
Mowat, Morden Maxwell	New Westminster, BC/ Campbellton
Mulherin, Louis Herbert	Grand Falls
Murray, James Wendell	Newcastle
Murray, Lloyd James	Moncton
Nase, Harold Fleming	Saint John
Nicholson, Frank Allen	St. Stephen
Norman, N. Roland	Sackville
O'Leary, Edward Launce	Richibucto
Orchard, William Harold	Chipman
Osborne, Hubert Patterson	Belleville, ON/Fredericton
Oulton, Arthur Everett Lockwood	Dorchester
Parks, Herbert Clifford	East Apple River, NS/ Butternut Ridge
Parlee, George William	Stanley
Parlee, Medley Kingdon	Stanley
Paterson, Robert Holder	Saint John
Patterson, John Blair Balfour	Saint John
Peacock, Ernest Frederick Woodham	Montreal/Saint John
Peacock, Hubert William	Montreal/Saint John
Peacock, Raymond Clinton	Rolling Dam Station
Perry, Fred	Florenceville
Pickle, Frank Lawrence	Bloomfield Station
Pitt, Harold Garfield	Saint John
Popplestone, John	Fredericton
Power, Frederick Edward	Saint John
Powers, John Fred	Saint John
Price, Everett Leslie	Moncton
Price, Harold Newton	Moncton
Price, John Warren	Moncton
Rankin, Franklin Sharp	Woodstock
Richard, Leo Lefebvre	Dorchester

Name	Birthplace/Residence
Richards, Joseph (French Air Force)	Molus River
Richardson, Leonard Atwood	Richardson, Deer Island/ Boston, MA
Ritchie, Elmer Tomas	Upper Kent
Richie, John Alexander	Saint John
Ritchie, Louis McCoskery	Saint John
Roberts, John Harold	Saint John
Rowley, John Whitfield	Saint John
Roy, Leo Patrick Joseph	St. Leonard
Russell, James Douglas	Russellville
Ryder, Frank Herbert	St. Stephen
Sands, Lloyd Allison	Moncton
Scott, Charles Walker	Saint John
Scovil, Earle Markee	St. Stephen
Scovil, Guy Dunning	Saint John
Shamper, Edgar	Kingston
Shives, Robert Kilgour	Campbellton
Sinclair, Rankine Murray	Saint John
Smith, Dean Melville Campbell	Moncton
Smith, Royden Morehouse	St. Stephen
Smith, Wellington Austin	Randolph
Soden, Frank Ormond	Petitcodiac/England
Steeves, Gordon Tracy	Surrey
Steeves, Omer Leon	Moncton/Albert Mines
Steeves, Verne William	Hillsboro
Stephenson, Alfred Edward	Saint John
Stevenson, Leigh Forbes	Bouctouche/Roblin, MB
Stewart, Alfred Patton	Woodstock
Stewart, Cecil Edwin	Woodstock
Stewart, Horace Cameron	St. George
Stockton, Ronald Picard	Saint John/Vancouver, BC
Sullivan, Herman Eagles	Saint John
Taylor, Gordon Winslow	Gagetown
Thornton, Arthur Campbell	Hartland
Tingley, Hartley Amos	Beaver Brook
Tompkins, Bradstreet	Florenceville
Travis, Frederick Pauley Joseph	Saint John
Trentowsky, Roland Ottomar	Saint John

Name	Birthplace/Residence
Trites, Stanley Bliss	Salisbury
Turner, Frederick Harold	Saint John
Wheeler, Wesley Allison	Athol
Whiteside, Arthur Barlow	Qu'Appelle, SK/Richibucto/ New Jerusalem
Williams, Thomas	Moncton
Wilson, Harold Edison	Chipman
Windsor, Byron Harper	Bathurst
Wisely, William Burton	Saint John
Wood, William Trueman	Sackville
Wootten, George Bates	Andover
Wright, Fleming Gordon	Campbellton/Petitcodiac
Wyse, Harry Ogilvie	Newcastle
Wyse, Robert Nicholson	Newcastle
Young, Frederick Carson	Caraquet

Acknowledgements

Thanks to the following: Marc Milner, who encouraged me to complete this book and edited the manuscript; freelance copy editor Barry Norris; and Alan Sheppard, managing editor, and Julie Scriver, creative director of Goose Lane Editions.

Michael Bechthold drew the maps and also shared information on Edward Cronin from his work on Raymond Collishaw.

Over the years I have worked on this project, I have received assistance from many people.

Kevin Anderson, director of the New Brunswick Aviation Museum, who contributed information from the museum's archives.

Patti Clark for her valuable assistance on Robert Shives.

Irene Doyle, who sent me information on Morden Mowat.

Annette Fulford, who offered her expertise on several airmen who married English war brides, especially Royden Foley, Harold Price, and James Vans McDonald.

Josh Green and Stephen Gregg from the Provincial Archives of New Brunswick, who provided photos from the archives.

Steve Harris and Hugh Halliday, who both sent important information from the Directorate of History Archives.

Melynda Jarratt of the New Brunswick Military History Museum for assistance on the Alvah Good Collection.

Shannyn Johnson from the Canadian War Museum, who helped with images.

Alena Krasnikova and Cynthia Wallace-Casey from the Fredericton Region Museum, who provided information on the museum's collections, especially that of Alvah Good.

François LeBlanc, who sent images from the Centre d'études acadiennes
Anselme-Chiasson, Université de Moncton

Jennifer Longon from the New Brunswick Museum, who provided photos
from the museum's collection.

Bridget Murphy at the Moncton Museum, who sent photos from the
museum's collection.

Roger Nason for information on Thomas Babbitt and John Fraser.

Beverley Plume for information on Stanley airmen, especially George and
Medley Parlee.

Margot and David Russell for information and photos on Louis Ritchie,
Margot's father, and Clair Gilmour.

Harold Wright provided information and photos on Edward Cronin and
Leigh Stevenson.

Selected Bibliography

Primary Sources
Archival

Centre d'études acadiennes Anselme-Chiasson, Université de Moncton

Alfred H. Belliveau Fonds no. 37. Autobiography. "Thoughts in Old Age" 37.1.3; "'Oh, Those Hungry Kriegsgefangeners!' Prisoners of War in Kaiser Wilhem's Deutschland in 1918," 37.1.4; "Working and retirement Years," 37.1.5.

Library and Archives Canada

CEF Personnel Files

New Brunswick Museum Archives

Rankin Family Papers

Charles Frederick Cawley Fonds

Provincial Archives of New Brunswick

G. Alvah Good Fonds, MC 300-MS 69

Haney, Heine Family Collection, MC 1999

Smith Family Fonds, MC 3622

The National Archives (UK)

British Royal Air Force, Airmen's Service Records, 1912-1939

International Committee of the Red Cross (ICRC) Archives

Printed

Carter, Lieutenant Weldon. "War in the Air." *University of New Brunswick Memorial Magazine* (1919): 50–54.

Richardson, Leonard Atwood. *Pilot's Log: The Flying Log, Diaries, Letters Home and Verse of Lt. Leonard Atwood Richardson Royal Flying Corps. WWI 1917-1918.* Compiled and edited by Elizabeth Richardson-Whealy. St. Catharines, ON: Paul Heron Publishing, 1998.

Secondary Sources

Bashow, David L. *Knights of the Air: Canadian Fighter Pilots in the First World War.* Toronto: McArthur, 2000.

Conrad, Peter C. *Training Aces: Canada's Air Training During the First World War.* Markham, ON: Bookland Press, 2015.

Franks, Norman, and Andy Saunders. *Mannock: The Life and Death of Major Edward Mannock VC DSO MC RAF.* London: Grub Street, 2008.

Godefroy, Andrew B. "From Gentleman Cadet to No Known Grave: The Life and Death of Lieutenant (Observer/Gunner) Franklin Sharp Rankin." *Canadian Air Force Journal* 1 no. 3 (Fall 2008): 11–19.

Hunt, C.W. *Dancing in the Sky: The Royal Flying Corps in Canada.* Toronto: Dundurn Press, 2009.

Philpott, Maryam. *Air and Sea Power in World War I: Combat and Experience in the Royal Flying Corps and the Royal Navy.* London: Bloomsbury Academic, 2013.

Rowinski, James, ed. *In Perpetuity: The First World War Soldiers of the Fredericton War Memorial.* Fredericton, NB: Goose Lane Editions and the Gregg Centre for the Study of War and Society, 2023.

Smith, John T. *Gone to Russia to Fight: The RAF in South Russia 1918–1920.* Chalford, UK: Amberley, 2010.

Taylor, Stewart K. "Unchecked Ego: Major Albert Desbrisay Carter, DSO, 19 Squadron RFC—Part 1." *Cross & Cockade International* 40 (Spring 2009): 3–31.

Taylor, Stewart K. "Dolphin Guru: Major Albert Desbrisay Carter, DSO, 19 Squadron RFC—Part 2." *Cross & Cockade International* 40 (Summer 2009): 88–108.

Taylor, Stewart K. "'Such a topping chap': 2Lt Morden Maxwell Mowat 23 Sqn RFC A Flt &11Sqn RFC B Flt, 1916." *Cross & Cockade International* 47 (Spring 2016): 3–9.

Wise, S.F. *Canadian Airmen and the First World War. The Official History of the Royal Canadian Air Force Volume 1.* Toronto: University of Toronto Press, 1980.

Website

"Major Albert Desbrisay Carter DSO in the Great War." CEFRG (Canadian Expeditionary Force Research Group) Blog, 2021. https://cefrg.ca/blog/major-albert-desbrisay-carter-dso/

Newspapers

Brantford Expositor

Campbellton Graphic

Carleton Observer

Carleton Sentinel

Daily Gleaner (Fredericton)

Daily Telegraph (Saint John)

Kings County Record (Sussex)

Moncton Daily Times

North Shore Leader (Newcastle)

Saint John Globe

St. John Standard

St. Croix Courier (St. Stephen)

INDEX

The New Brunswick Military Heritage Project

The New Brunswick Military Heritage Project, a non-profit organization devoted to public awareness of the remarkable military heritage of the province, is an initiative of the Brigadier Milton F. Gregg, VC, Centre for the Study of War and Society of the University of New Brunswick. The organization consists of museum professionals, teachers, university professors, graduate students, active and retired members of the Canadian Forces, and other historians. We welcome public involvement. People who have ideas for books or information for our database can contact us through our website: www.unb.ca/nbmhp.

One of the main activities of the New Brunswick Military Heritage Project is the publication of the New Brunswick Military Heritage Series with Goose Lane Editions. This series of books is under the direction of J. Brent Wilson, Director of the New Brunswick Military Heritage Project at the University of New Brunswick. Publication of the series is supported by the Province of New Brunswick and the Canadian War Museum.

The New Brunswick Military Heritage Series

War among the Clouds is volume 31 in the New Brunswick Military
Heritage Series. For a full list of books in the series, see:
https://gooselane.com/collections/new-brunswick-military-heritage-series

About the Author

J. Brent Wilson worked at the Centre for Conflict Studies and the Brigadier Milton F. Gregg, VC, Centre for the Study of War and Society at the University of New Brunswick from 1989 until 2024. He was Director of the New Brunswick Military Heritage Project and Editor Emeritus of the New Brunswick Military Heritage Book Series. He taught military history in UNB's Department of History from 1988 to 2021. He has conducted battlefield tours in France, Belgium, Canada, and the United States with the Canadian Battlefields Foundation, the Canadian Armed Forces, and commercial tour companies. His publications include *Hurricane Pilot: The Wartime Letters of Harry L. Gill, DFM, 1940–1943* (2007); *Kandahar Tour: The Turning Point in Canada's Afghan Mission* (2008); *Loyal Gunners: 3rd Field Artillery Regiment (The Loyal Company) and the History of New Brunswick Artillery, 1893 to 2012* (2016); and *A Family of Brothers: Soldiers of the 26th New Brunswick Battalion in the Great War* (2018).